ALL THINGS NEW

Starting Where Jesus Finished

Chuck Elmore

ACKNOWLEDGEMENTS

For all the ways their influence has directed my steps and contributed to the writing of this book, I would like to express my deepest gratitude to:

Gary Elmore, for being my most constant example of a godly man, for being a worker approved who accurately handles the word of truth, and for being a loving, affirming, and encouraging father. Becky tells me I look more and more like you as the days go by, and that blesses me.

Dale Griffin and Bruce Robertson, for devoting seasons in your lives to helping students lay foundations for Kingdom living, for declaring that Jesus is enough, and for living out the grace you so diligently taught.

Pastors Alan and Gail Hawkins, for countless ways you've sown blessings into my life and spoken healing words into my heart, and for all the sacrifices you've made to give Jesus a place to lay His head. Thank you, Alan, for pushing me to finish this book.

Gary Archibeck, for invaluable critiques and feedback that sharpened this message, and for powerful words of affirmation and encouragement.

Ben Stewart, for your generous and unexpected assistance with helping this book take form and shape.

Jenny Hammit for many years of friendship, and for your proofreading expertise.

Bryan Ryder, for your years as a sounding board for these insights, for questions and answers, and for picking up the Gospel torch and running with it.

Bob George, Clifton Coulter, Barry Manson, Andrew Wommack, Paul Ellis, Steve McVey, Andrew Farley, and numerous other Gospel preachers for instruction and inspiration.

Tom, Sherry, and Caleb Green and Emiel Ross, for numbering me among your tribe, for your faithfulness to the Gospel, for years of laughter, music, and Mexican food, and for preaching, praying, and modeling a message that changed my life. Tom, so much of what I've received from you is in this book.

Becky Elmore, for loving me selflessly, for praying me through nights of doubt, for lifting my eyes, for your tenderness, affection, and companionship, and for the shelter I find in you.

Maggie, Lillie, and Faye for amplifying and expanding what I know of Abba's love, and for the joy of watching you walk with Him. I love you all so much!

God the Father, Jesus the Son, and the Holy Spirit, for abundant, eternal, new creation life, for perfect love, for forgiveness, for communion, for Your presence, for Your sacrifice, for Your voice, for bringing me out of the tomb with You, and for grace.

I would also like to acknowledge my special fondness and deep appreciation for the Apostle Paul, his ministry, and his writings. As you will see through dozens of Pauline scripture references throughout this book, God has used his epistles to greatly illuminate my understanding of the Good News of Jesus Christ, which, of course, was the point.

Special thanks to all of you who, after hearing me teach, preach, or converse on this, my life message, urged me to commit it to writing. Thank you for your patience, and may you be blessed.

And thank you to my beautiful church family at New Life City. Thank you for your love, words, and expressions of encouragement through the years. I am so grateful to be walking with you.

CONTENTS

Dedicated in Loving Memory…

To my mother, Suzanne Sharp, the president of my fan club, the constant voice in my ear telling me how marvelous I was to her, the jeweler with the magnifying glass seeing the hidden value in me others didn't see. When I remember her relentless affirmation, encouragement, love, and rebukes when necessary, I remember the heart of Abba for His children. If you weren't blessed with a mother like mine, I pray this book helps you receive Abba's heart of grace toward you. He is the source of the glorious attributes my mother possessed.

To Barbara Martin, a woman so filled to overflowing with the Holy Spirit that I often felt terrified and safe around her at the same time. Barbara's love for the Lord and willingness to be a conduit for His power blessed and changed many lives, mine included.

To Rocky Green, a dear friend who changed my life as none other has. I will always give thanks to God for the love Rocky showed me from the first day we met. He most certainly detected my initial religiosity and saw the signs that I was living in my own strength and not living in the grace of Christ, yet he didn't get impatient with me or try to shame or berate me into the Kingdom. He looked at me like Jesus looked at Zacchaeus, and his kind-heartedness, graciousness, and love eventually brought about true repentance and opened my ears to hear the Good News I now joyfully proclaim.

Thank you all for showing me Jesus. Rest in peace.

FOREWORD

Everyone is writing about grace these days. It is as if some undiscovered treasure has been rescued from the bottom of the deepest sea. The mystery of the Spirit of revelation is that He often speaks to the church in many places at once. So it is unsurprising when so many hearers rise to tell us what the Spirit is saying to the church in a particular hour. The Spirit of God will always bring the body of Christ into greater hearing of the Gospel. We need these fresh understandings of grace as well as more profound experiences of our God that we might convey to the world this treasure. In your hands you have a valuable rethinking of these things.

The soft-spoken student who graced our home over twenty years ago has become a thunderous voice in the discussion about how God's love is mediated into our lives. *All Things New* will surprise and challenge you but a patient reception will bring you into good pasture. The young man I knew paid the price of conscience and rejection to simply express the thoughts which were the seed bed of this text. His willingness to be misunderstood, rejected and cast away has paid invaluable dividends. To imbibe these truths will be life changing.

Don't be surprised if the assertions of this book make you angry. Neither be surprised if your anger is the passage through the wardrobe into a whole new world. The goodness of God offends the mind. We all want justice administered to others and mercy to ourselves. Were this book written by one who has lived riotously it would come across as self-serving but it is written by one who's path is admirable. A wicked man receiving grace is a story we all easily understand and applaud but a good man being the object of God's boundless mercy shocks us. My wife always says that her husband was saved from a life of unrighteousness while she was rescued from a world of self-righteousness. The author of *All Things New* is a good man gone grace. Go with him.

Dr. Alan Hawkins
Senior Pastor, New Life City
Albuquerque, New Mexico

Chapter 1
ENOUGH ABOUT ME

On the day I met Jesus I was a sinner. I was marked by infidelity, transgression, and rebellion. I was a traitor, a stray, and a prodigal. I was unclean. I was faithless. I constantly missed the mark, and I was born that way. I was born with a curse on my head and a debt I could never pay. I recognized my weakness and exhausted what strength I had to expunge it, yet my weakness remained.

To the casual observer I was a model of virtue. There were no obvious indications of iniquity, no scars of consequence, and no clues pointing to a life shrouded in darkness. By comparison I was faring better than most as I abstained from the vices that shackled others, but I was a sinner nonetheless.

Some will dismiss this verdict as self-indictment reached through a sense of religious guilt or derived from an antiquated moralistic ideology, but the proof was locked up inside me. I bore the evidence in thoughts of despair, in a deep dissatisfaction with my condition, in the hollowness of life without divine communion, and in a yearning for acceptance and significance, for love and purpose.

On the day I met Jesus I was a sinner. Then I realized I was a dead man. I was killed--crucified with Christ, to be precise. That nature, that man, that identity was laid to rest. The Lord in

9

His grace chose to bring me out of the tomb along with Jesus as new creation, a member of a new race altogether, acquired through a second birth. I was washed clean by His blood. I was declared to be "in the right" with God through faith in His Son. I was filled with the Holy Spirit. His strength was made perfect in my weakness. My identity changed from sinner to saint, set apart for holy purpose.

If you're a child of God, this is your identity as well. In these pages, I want to offer hope to those brought to desperation by the condemnation of the Old Covenant. I want to point to Jesus those who are tired and heavy-laden and desperately needing rest. I want us to take a closer look at what we believe about the law and sin and confession and forgiveness and atonement. I want to highlight the futility of using the strength and wisdom of man to attain victories in the Kingdom of God. I want to point out that the more time we spend in supposed self-improvement, the less time we devote to Kingdom establishment, and the longer the world languishes in the grave while we try and solve for ourselves problems that Jesus solved with perfect finality on the cross and through the empty tomb.

Today, I walk in these truths with unwavering confidence in Jesus, but coming to this place of faith has been a long journey from the day that sinner was killed by grace. The process from that day to this has been to believe and receive who I Am says I am and to be transformed by the renewing of my mind. What follows, in brief, are all points in between.

From That Day to This

The son of a preacher man I am. My earliest memories were formed in a little Baptist church on the outskirts of Midland, Texas. My father, Gary Elmore, pastored this church until I was about five years old when circumstances led him to look for another vocation to support my mother, my older sister, my younger brother, and me. He began a long career in the semiconductor industry, a job that would have our family moving from town to town throughout Texas (and a glorious spell in Washington state) on average every three years. Throughout this season he also preached from time to time, helping various churches with a pastoral vacancy. Although Daddy no longer pastored full-time, he made it a point to find a church wherever we lived, and we faithfully attended weekly services, twice on Sunday and once on Wednesday night.

West Texas is not known for its scenery, but the flat, barren landscape of my childhood never seemed ugly to me. I was rather drawn to it. I superimposed its imagery onto the Bible stories I heard of godly men coming to maturity in the wilderness. I could close my eyes and see Moses, David, Jesus, and Paul earnestly seeking God on the same desolate earth as me. I could even picture Moses talking to the Lord through a burning Mesquite tree, though as dry as Midland was I had to use more imagination to see Jesus walking on water.

I had a tangible hunger for God at a young age, fostered by the strong faith of my parents. I remember a sweet season when Daddy would call us kids into the living room each night before bedtime to read Bible stories, and I absorbed and visualized every word about Jesus and His teachings and miracles. I remember Mama praying for me, encouraging me, and reminding me that I was the righteousness of God in Christ Jesus. Though my young mind could not fully comprehend her prayers, my spirit felt the weight of those words. I would look at the stars in the broad Texas sky and contemplate the heavens and the life that waited after this one ended. When I was seven years old, Mama and Daddy led me in a prayer to give my life to Jesus and to receive His life in return.

At twelve years of age, living again in Midland after several years away, I sensed God communicating to me. At least a half-dozen times over the course of a few weeks, I had thoughts, urgings, and impressions about being a minister. One Sunday morning while I watched my dad water the lawn before church, he asked me a question.

"Son, has the Lord been speaking to you?"

"Daddy, I think He has been. I think He wants me to be in the ministry."

I saw tears form in my father's eyes. With a nod of assurance he said, "He's been telling me the same thing." That morning, he walked with me down the aisle to tell the pastor of my decision to dedicate my life to ministry.

I am now into my forties, and I have called the high desert of New Mexico my home for over twenty years. My love for the desert has not changed, but my understanding of being a disciple of Christ has. For much of my Christian life I made lists and followed rules. If the expectations were written in black and white, it eliminated the guesswork and made it easier to please people and stay in the right. My love for the Lord was such that I didn't want to disappoint Him, so I was relieved to learn from pastors, mentors, and other Christians along the way that the path of righteousness was clearly marked with task-bearing signposts. Faithful church attendance? Check. Daily Bible-reading? Check. Sunday school lesson studied? Check. Tithing? Cash, when my parents handed me some loose change to drop into the plate. The way to stay on God's good side, as I understood it, was through a steadfast performance of these tasks. As a child and young man, I clung to godly performance as the singular trait that set me apart from my peers.

Through grade school, middle school, and most of high school, I was always the smallest boy in my class (and smaller than most of the girls, too). I didn't hit my growth spurt until my junior year in high school, and being small came with undesirable side effects. It meant getting picked last for games during PE and recess. It also meant garnering all the unwanted roles when acting out episodes of late 70's television shows with my buddies on the playground (Roscoe P. Coltrane if we were playing *The Dukes of Hazzard*, Twiki if we were playing *Buck Rogers in the 25th Century*, Officer Grossman if we were playing CHiPS). My fear and loathing of mathematics, and all sciences involving math, kept me from being a standout student, and none of the girls were interested in me in a romantic way. After all, what self-respecting girl would want to be seen with a guy she could out-lift on the bench press? I felt I needed to find other meaningful ways to prove myself and define my identity. Where did I excel? Piety. Following God's rules. And steadfast I was, all the way through childhood and through my teen years. Granted, it did not win me much respect at the schools I attended, but I was a true standout at church, and I was convinced that I was on God's honor roll.

I joined the United States Air Force after graduating from high school in 1989. After the late growth season I was now standing tall at just over 6 feet. I had a lot of growing to do yet, weighing in at just 123 pounds. My recruiter had to bend the rules so I could enlist, as I was a few pounds shy of the minimum required weight for my height. He advised me to eat a lot of cookies.

Mama was very worried about my enlistment, fearing the negative aspects of military life might lead me into temptation. Her worries proved to be unfounded (or more likely her prayers availed much), as I had a reputation for being a squeaky-clean fanatic. I was even dubbed "Brother Elmore" by my classmates at my technical training school after I protested the instructing sergeant's use of profanity. I attended services at the chapel or at churches off base, and I would always omit the word "hell" when singing the Air Force song in basic training, since I could only justify using the word "hell" when speaking geographically.

My performance-based approach to the Christian life was humming along nicely until I had a souring experience while stationed in Southern Italy during the first Gulf War. I had befriended a female coworker a few years older than me who'd had a baby prior to marriage. Typically, as a judgmental and self-righteous churchgoer, I would have kept the likes of her at arms-length, but she had shown me kindness and looked after me like a big sister when I was the new guy, and I really enjoyed her friendship. She won my heart by giving me a towel that Irish rock band U2's lead singer Bono used to mop his brow during a concert, along with an enormous movie poster of U2's *Rattle and Hum*. I attended a church off base for American military personnel, and I decided to invite her. When she walked in with me one Sunday she received a few surprised stares from people who knew her. I even recall one man's look of disdain. She shifted a little uncomfortably but soldiered on bravely through the singing and the sermon. Then came communion. When the deacons came by with the bread and the grape juice (unfermented, of course), they deliberately skipped her. Her eyes grew wide with shock while my face grew hot with embarrassment and indignation. As soon as the service concluded, she headed straight for the door, and I followed right behind.

For the first time I started to question the things I believed. I started to carry offense in my heart towards the church in general. I felt like my connection with God was fine, and that my withdrawal from church was even endorsed by Him, because certainly He wouldn't be party to such shameful treatment of others, though in the church's defense, they sincerely believed excluding my friend from communion was to protect her from eating and drinking damnation upon herself. Even still, I entered a time of dissension. I rejected the strictures of my upbringing and went through a bit of a rebellion, mild though it was (I started smoking cigars and listening to rock and roll).

By the time my enlistment was over, I was ready to give the church another chance. I moved to a different wilderness and made my home in Albuquerque. As a student at the University of New Mexico, I became heavily involved with the Baptist Student Union. I can freely admit now my motives were not pure in coming back to church life. In all honesty, I arrived with a plan to get the acclaim and acceptance I never had in my younger days, poised to win the young campus ministry crowd over as a Bible-thumping Jesus lover who had seen the world, fought in a war, and smoked a few stogies to boot. To add to the mystique, I carried around my guitar and started playing with the worship team. In my estimation, I was now the cat's meow.

In just a short amount of time, I found the things I prided myself in to be worthless. As I listened to the words of ministry director Dale Griffin, I was confronted again and again by the liberating message of the grace of God and the recurring theme that nothing I did or had to offer could make God love me any more or any less. This was a fundamental building block that holds up in my life to this day. Dale lovingly addressed the instability of any foundation that did not include Jesus, or that included Jesus plus other things. Dale's mantra was "Jesus plus anything else is religion. Jesus is enough." Bruce Robertson, one of the ministry assistants, and still one of my heroes, also mentored me through this period of growth and genuine maturity.

Under the guidance of Dale and Bruce I grew to believe that all my efforts, striving, accomplishments, and works could never impress God, nor change the vastness of His love for me, but I couldn't escape the fact that I could still impress other people, and I found myself constantly craving that approval. With graciousness and patience, those men taught me of the emptiness of living as a whitewashed tomb, the description Jesus used for those who looked good on the outside but were dead on the inside. Dale and Bruce also started me on the journey of finding my identity and worth in Christ alone.

While at the BSU, I met and fell in love with Becky Sue Smith, the woman who would become my wife and mother of our three daughters. I was drawn to her natural beauty, but also to her compassion and humility. She was a friend to the outcast and a cheerleader for the underdog. Her laugh was musical and heartfelt, and she loved the Lord. I fell for her in a big way.

Becky was the first woman I passionately kissed, and along with those passionate kisses came a new affront to my steadfast ways in the form of a powerful force set on exerting its dominion over my thoughts and physical desires in ways I had never faced before. My years of piety and my lack of romantic relationships had been a shelter from physical temptation, and for that, I am grateful to God. But now, my drive had come alive, and I found myself woefully underprepared to deal with it.

When I confided my struggle with my college buddies, they were shocked that I was entering the war with sexual temptation at such a late age, a war they had fought since middle school or before. Though I was a virgin when I married Becky, I found myself ill equipped to contend with my physical desires. Using the meager weapons of willpower, behavioral rules, and the knowledge of good and evil, I lost many personal battles with lust and temptation before marriage. Those defeats plunged me into previously foreign feelings of doubt, guilt, shame, and an unshakeable thought that I had lost God's favor. I was certainly off the honor roll.

The advice from friends, elders, and pastors was always the same. When you fail, confess your sin to the Lord and ask Him to forgive you. He is faithful and just to do so. Of course,

I knew this advice already. I had memorized 1 John 1:9 years ago, and I used it like scriptural antacid anytime I had sin-induced heartburn. I had given the same advice to others on numerous occasions. It gave me a small amount of relief at first, but to my growing dismay and consternation, *it did not curb my appetite.* In fact, my appetite increased!

What could have been a beautiful season of trust and growth between Becky, me and Jesus instead became a routine of giving in to temptation, confessing my sin and asking forgiveness, and assuring Jesus I would never do it again. Relational growth was stunted between Becky and me since I became so consumed by the physical aspect of our relationship. Growth was also stunted in my friendship with Jesus since I believed He wanted nothing to do with me until I got my act together. This, of course, was an effective lie of the Enemy that created distance in my mind between my Savior and me. The failures became more frequent, and over time my assurances to the Lord became less emphatic, until I found myself asking Him for forgiveness while plotting my next transgression. What I believed to be repentance was not in fact a turning away from the things that hurt me, but merely a shallow expression of remorse induced by guilt and shame. I did not truly repent, but rather only collapsed on the road of my ruin until my guilt wore off and my pain abated. Then I stood again and resumed my walk on the path of destruction.

The voice of the Accuser grew louder in my head as I started to believe my life was a sham, my faith was worthless, and my credibility with the Lord was shot to hell. I felt I needed to engage in acts of penitence to prove to God I was sorry. The Devil had me convinced that God's grace was quickly running out and I needed to prove myself worthy of an extension by working harder. I felt God's grace was there for occasional stumbling, but surely not for this habitual sin. Eventually, penitence gave way to bitterness as I began to view God as an unreasonable taskmaster with impossible demands. I began to believe His approval was unattainable. I began to doubt His love. I began to walk in rejection.

Is this your story? Is it the story of someone you know? Does this cycle sound familiar to you? The disappointment I felt in letting God down was compounded by the fact that I'd lived all my life without these kinds of struggles. No amount of Bible-reading, church attendance, quiet times, evangelism, or tithing could erase the disgust and shame I felt. I found these efforts brought little comfort, as they now more than ever felt like a debt owed from a bankrupt soul. In my despondency I found myself returning again and again to the only comfort I could find, the brief respite from misery that habitual sin provides. When the thrill was gone, the pit I'd fallen into had deepened. But where sin abounded, grace abounded all the more!

In the midst of this most troubling period of my life, the hand of the Lord lifted me up out of the pit and set my feet upon a Rock. It began while serving with a college summer missions team in Fort Sumner, New Mexico when I met the Greens, a family that God would use mightily in my life. Tom and Sherry, roughly the same age as my parents, were Gospel ministers who used their tremendous musical talents as a vehicle to present the Good News in churches all over. Their three children, daughter Emiel and sons Rocky and Caleb, were musical as well and truly delightful to be around. I was quickly drawn to Rocky, who was close to my age and shared a lot of common interests.

Rocky was unlike anyone I had ever met. He wowed me right off with his vast musical virtuosity. He sang and wrote songs, played guitar, drums, bass, keys, saxophone, mandolin, harmonica, and the list goes on. He told tales of growing up a surfer in Florida, and he drew me in deeper with a big smile, an easy laugh, and a brilliant sense of humor. He had long, blond hair and was barefoot most of the time. Everything about him spoke of freedom, especially his journey with Jesus and how obviously Rocky's life reflected a powerful communion with Him. He would get emotional with wonder and gratitude while recounting conversations he'd had with the Lord. Rocky and I grew close in brotherhood and in myriad ways our hearts were knit together as I got to know him and his family. His companionship also helped take my mind off my personal struggles.

Then came the wilderness epiphany. Moses had one, Paul had one, and by God, so did I. One weekend in February of 1996, in the desert outside of Fort Sumner I found hope again. I had come to town to see Tom, Rocky, and Caleb perform as a jazz trio for a Valentine's Day banquet. The music was sweet, but it was just the start of an even sweeter weekend. The next night Tom called us into the living room for a Bible study. He read out of Hebrews, specifically spending a lot of time in chapters 8, 9, and 10. I started hearing things about the complete sufficiency of Jesus' sacrifice in dealing with sin, about the thorough and final cleansing power of His blood. I heard things that seemed too good to be true, and naturally I countered this good news with questions from my experience to the contrary. Tom, Sherry, and Rocky took turns answering my despairing queries with the grace, love, and hope of Jesus. That day began a journey of revelation and discovery for me, but more than that, the beginning of an end to religious bondage in my life, religion that did nothing to heal my problem. Along that journey, I jettisoned some unhealthy and misguided beliefs and exchanged them for Gospel truth.

The epiphany changed the course of my life in more ways than one as it came shortly after I was licensed and ordained in the Southern Baptist denomination. As I grew in my understanding of Jesus' atoning victory over sin, I realized key elements of my beliefs did not line up with the doctrine of the church I served as youth pastor. I shared my change of heart with my youth leaders. When it came to light, the church leadership questioned me about it on several occasions and found me unwilling to budge, so they asked me to resign. I completely understand their decision. I drew a hard line that contradicted some of their beliefs, and I had not yet learned how to appeal to my brothers and sisters with grace and love. Leaving the church was painful. I lost friends, I lost credibility, and I disappointed mentors whom I love and respect to this day. But I gained a revelation of God's goodness in my life, for the first time in my life, and of the finality of Christ's work on the cross. The renewing of my mind has resulted in a Holy Spirit-led transformation in me that continues to this day.

After leaving the denomination in which I grew up, it was not long before Tom, Sherry, Becky, and I talked about starting a home church in Albuquerque. My dad was all for it and wanted the church to meet in his home. We launched Albuquerque Grace Fellowship and had a blessed season of worship, prayer, and unabashed Gospel preaching, focusing on the finished work of Christ and our identity as Kingdom citizens in new creation living in the glorious New Covenant with God. This season lasted for over five years and then it came to a close. It felt like it was time for something more, for an increase in operating in the power of the Holy Spirit, though it pained Becky and me to see our home church end. When I expressed to Rocky my mixed feelings about this particular time of ministry being over, he responded with some of his trademark surfer wisdom. "The Lord sent you a beautiful wave, man, and you rode it all the way in to shore. It's time to paddle out and wait for the next one."

The next wave was a season of learning and growth as Becky and I learned more about the presence of God and the fullness of the Holy Spirit. Tom and Sherry prayed for our baptism in the Holy Spirit, and God touched both of us in a powerful way. We searched around Albuquerque for a church to attend and spent some sweet time in charismatic circles and a few Vineyard churches. We finally ended up at the church of Alan and Gail Hawkins, mentors and friends who had also come from a Southern Baptist ministry background. Alan counseled Becky and me before we were married and he prayed a blessing over us in our wedding. Alan and Gail pastored a church called New Life City. We quickly discovered it was a church that loved the presence of God, loved the nations, and loved each other. During the first few weeks of attending New Life City, Becky and I would weep from the sweetness of God's presence in the room. It was something we had not experienced so powerfully before. We knew we were home.

I now serve at New Life City as an associate pastor, and I see the ways I have grown since being a part of this church. I have come to understand more fully my role as an ambassador of the Kingdom of God, and I understand that my power is from His indwelling Holy Spirit. I am learning to hear God's voice. I am learning to wield weapons that are not carnal but rather are of the Spirit and are mighty for the pulling down of strongholds, and I am teaching others to do so.

In retrospect, I see that my journey to a place of confidence in and communion with Jesus took so long because I had entered the wrong coordinates into my Godliness Positioning System. I was trying to reach the destination of righteousness, holiness, and forgiveness when that had been my place of origin from the moment of salvation! It is *from* an origin of righteousness, holiness, and forgiveness that the real journey begins. "Behold," Jesus says, "I make all things new." Starting there, the journey is full of worship and wonder, communion and commission, and the destination is seeing Jesus face to face, knowing Him as He knows us. Of course, my journey continues, but I want to share with you what I have learned so far with the prayer that it can help those of you stuck in the wearying cycle of performance, striving, sin, and despair and see you restored to hope and full reliance on the Lord. My deepest hope for you as you read this book is that it will point you to the transforming truths of the Gospel of grace.

Please know that while some may find the views contained in these pages controversial, I am not trying to pick fights or subvert denominations or establish new doctrines, and I am far from being the only one to believe or teach this message of grace (praise be to God). We are urged by the Apostle Paul in 1 Thessalonians 5:21 to test everything and hold on to what is good. After years of believing what I was told without hesitation, I have been vigorously testing what I believe for over twenty years now. I have discovered that God is not afraid of my questions and that the truth bears up under even the most intense scrutiny.

I do not need or expect you to agree with everything in this book, but my hope for you as you read it is that you will challenge traditions and beliefs you have held to be true, and that in testing things, you will come to a new appreciation of who you are in Christ and the abundant life you've been called to live. I pray that you will be transformed by the renewing of your mind, and I know firsthand that this transformation will empower you to proclaim the Good News like never before. I pray that as you push past the veil of legalistic mistruths, you will behold the face of God.

In 2009, Rocky passed into the eternal presence of Jesus after complications from brain cancer took his life. He was 34 years old and never got the chance to see or hold his baby girl Evangeline, born to his wife Jena just 4 months later. The deep and temporal ache that abides will one day be swallowed up in victory. Rocky's death reignited in me a passionate desire to spread the good news of the marvelous love, grace, and resurrection life of Jesus.

I'm happy to say my dad is doing what he loves and is pastoring again. Since 2007, he has proclaimed the Gospel to a loving and devoted congregation of saints in Kodiak, Alaska. I, too, am blessed to be living out my ministry calling, serving alongside my gracious and empowering pastors and our amazing family at New Life City. It's an absolute joy to see people, including my wife and three daughters, thrive in such a grace-filled, Spirit-led environment, and my hope grows daily as I see the Kingdom of God established in a lost and hopeless world.

Okay. Enough about me. Let's look at Jesus.

Chapter 2.
THE OLDEST TRICK IN THE BOOK

Grace and truth came through Jesus Christ. Jesus came to show us the face of God. He came to speak with the voice of God. He came to forgive, heal, and restore with the love of God. He came to destroy the works of the Devil. He came to reverse the curse on humanity and on creation. He came as the one prophesied, the seed of the woman who would crush the head of the serpent. Jesus came to overcome death with life, to overcome sin with grace, to replace the sorrowful isolation of humankind with restored fellowship to the triune God. His triumph came through humble suffering, laying down His rights as God.

We see the Lord's original intent for us in Genesis. We see God give man peace, provision, acceptance, significance, and fellowship. We see the Trinity give man a companion from his own flesh and bone after recognizing that it was not good for man to be alone. We see the Lord place the man and the woman in the midst of His wondrous creation with the directive to "be fruitful and multiply, fill the earth, and subdue it." We were made for community and communion, for intimate sharing and exchange with Father, Son, and Holy Spirit.

The Enemy

We also see the Enemy's plan in Genesis, revealed in

chapter 3. Knowing that God is the source of all life, the Enemy repeatedly resorts to the oldest trick in the book: persuading us to take our eyes off the Lord. If we do not experience every aspect of life and creation in fellowship and communion with the Lord, we not only miss the fullness of existence, we become susceptible to deceit, decay, and death. When the Enemy succeeds in diverting our attention from the Lord, he also disrupts our bond with our fellow man and stirs strife and hostility between us. The Enemy employs a number of tactics to reach his goal of diversion, as we see in this revealing and pivotal scripture passage:

1 "Now the serpent was more crafty than any other beast of the field that the Lord God had made. He said to the woman, "Did God actually say, 'You shall not eat of any tree in the garden?'" 2 And the woman said to the serpent, "We may eat of the fruit of the trees in the garden, 3 but God said, 'You shall not eat of the fruit of the tree that is in the midst of the garden, neither shall you touch it, lest you die.'" 4 But the serpent said to the woman, "You will not surely die. 5 For God knows that when you eat of it your eyes will be opened, and you will be like God, knowing good and evil." 6 So when the woman saw that the tree was good for food, and that it was a delight to the eyes, and that the tree was to be desired to make one wise, she took of its fruit and ate, and she also gave some to her husband who was with her, and he ate. 7 Then the eyes of both were opened, and they knew that they were naked. And they sewed fig leaves together and made themselves loincloths." Genesis 3:1-7

For the sake of better understanding, I will preface my exposition of this passage with a brief discussion of this Enemy we face. What do we know about Satan from scripture? Passages in Isaiah, Ezekiel, and Daniel suggest he was once a member of the heavenly host and that he was beautiful and wise. Isaiah 14:13-14 attributes this quote to Satan (when he was known as Lucifer):

"I will ascend into heaven, I will exalt my throne above the stars of God; I will also sit on the mount of the congregation on the farthest sides of the north; I will ascend above the heights of the clouds, I will be like the Most High."

God responded to Lucifer's pride and self-exaltation in Ezekiel 28:15-17:

"You were perfect in your ways from the day you were created, till iniquity was found in you. By the abundance of your trading you became filled with violence within, and you sinned; therefore I cast you as a profane thing out of the mountain of God; and I destroyed you, O covering cherub, from the midst of the fiery stones. Your heart was lifted up because of your beauty; you corrupted your wisdom for the sake of your splendor; I cast you to the ground, I laid you before kings, that they might gaze at you."

While we lack a comprehensive scriptural narrative of the fall of Satan, we know that he became intoxicated with his own beauty and splendor to the point of compromising his God-given wisdom. In arrogance he sought equality with God, in stark contrast to Jesus, who did not see equality with God as something to demand or cling to (Philippians 2:6). Lucifer was cast down, and it has been his aim since then to corrupt the goodness of God's creation. The name Satan means "adversary" in Hebrew. The name devil means "false accuser, slanderer" in Greek. He has come to steal, kill, and destroy. He is the father of lies. He is the Accuser of the brethren.

The Enemy's Schemes

Genesis 3:1-12 exposes the schemes of the Enemy. The same tactics Satan (as the serpent) used against Eve he continues to employ today. Instead of us keeping our eyes on our loving God, Satan wants us to:

1) Put our eyes on the command (Gen. 3:1)

2) Put our eyes on a lie (Gen. 3:4)

3) Put our eyes on our lack (Gen. 3:5)

4) Put our eyes on temptation (Gen. 3:6)

5) Put our eyes on our shame (Gen. 3:7)

6) Put our eyes on each other (Gen. 3:12)

In Adam and Eve's case, Satan used all six of these tactics sequentially, but he is not confined to this order or this number. In general, this sequence is commonly experienced whenever we submit to temptation, but the Enemy can succeed at taking our eyes from Jesus with even one of these tactics, if we are listening to his voice and not the voice of our Good Shepherd. Throughout the remaining chapters of this book, I will address these tactics in greater detail, but I will first offer a quick overview of each.

In the Beginning

The story of creation was unfolding beautifully. God created the heavens, the earth, and all that is in it, and because His desire was for fellowship, He created man. He gave man food, work, and companionship. Sustenance, significance, and acceptance, everything a human needs.

Paradise was short-lived. A diabolical menace entered this idyllic setting, described as a serpent in the third chapter of Genesis, and this Enemy, seeking to remove man's eyes from their Father, spoke his first words to man. These, like all his words to follow, began with a distortion of the words of God.

Eyes on the Command - "Did God really say you couldn't eat from *any* of the trees in this garden?" Eve, whose mind sin had not yet tainted, instantly saw the foolishness of this question. No, as a matter of fact, God did *not* say that. God's plan was not rampant prohibition but abundant provision.

"We may eat of the fruit of the trees in the garden," she answered. "All except for one. If we eat of the tree in the midst of the garden, or even touch it, we will die." But look what the crafty serpent accomplished with this question; he put Eve's eyes on the *one and only* tree in the garden from which she was warned not to eat, and had called to mind the law. We, like Eve, usually combat the initial lie of the Enemy by reciting the law that tells us what we cannot do. In doing so, we ensnare ourselves in the trap described in Romans 7:7-11:

"What then shall we say? That the law is sin? By no means! Yet if it had not been for the law, I would not have known sin. For I would not have known what it is to covet if the law had not said, 'You shall not covet.' But sin, seizing an opportunity through the commandment, produced in me all kinds of covetousness. For apart from the law, sin lies dead. I was once alive apart from the law, but when the commandment came, sin came alive and I died. The very commandment that promised life proved to be death to me. For sin, seizing an opportunity through the commandment, deceived me and through it killed me."

With Eve's mind on the law, the Enemy then attempted to undermine her trust in God and get her to question His motives.

Eyes on a Lie - The serpent's next step was to convince Eve that God was not being honest with her. "You won't die. God only said that because he knows what will really happen. You will become like him, knowing good and evil." This series of lies subtly shifted Eve's attention from what she knew to be true about God and introduced the question, "Can God be trusted?"

Compounding the problem for us today is that the world

fell into brokenness as Adam and Eve surrendered their God-given dominion to the Enemy. In the midst of this brokenness, we are told again and again that if God were loving, powerful, and trustworthy, He wouldn't allow evil and suffering to exist. In response to this lie, I say that God didn't allow it. We did. Dominion was ours and we traded it for forbidden fruit. What remains in paradise lost is a hard-scrabble existence where deceived humans try to get what they can while they can. The Enemy is all too happy to offer inferior substitutes to fill the void for the life-giving provision that only comes from the Lord.

Eyes on Our Lack - Not only had God kept Eve in the dark, according to the serpent, but He had withheld good things from her. As doubt crept into Eve's mind, she began to question what she was missing. She didn't possess the knowledge of good and evil, and now she felt deficient because of it. So much of the power of temptation comes from us believing we don't have what we need. We often don't have what we want, but trusting the Lord means trusting Him with our lack, and waiting for provision to come from His hand, not from ours or the Enemy's. But waiting is not easy for us, especially when the Enemy puts our eyes on the object of our desires.

Eyes on Temptation - Eve bought the lie. She felt her lack. She looked at the fruit. Instead of taking a 360-degree survey of all the other permissible trees that surrounded her and offered true goodness and sustaining nourishment, she looked at the fruit from the singular tree that was off the menu. And in looking, she saw that it was pleasant to the eyes and desirable for the wisdom it was said to possess. She forgot about God's lovingkindness. She doubted God's warning. She questioned God's trustworthiness. She ate, and she gave some to Adam, who also ate.

Let us take care not to cast stones here. How many of us have said or thought in moments of self-righteousness that we would have rejected the forbidden fruit? And yet, we daily eat the fruit of self-reliance while standing in the vast orchard of God's provision.

What follows the appearance of the Enemy as tempter is his most insidious incarnation, the Accuser.

Eyes on Our Shame - We do not hear the Devil bring an accusation against Adam and Eve, but we see them scramble for fig leaves as they felt the shame and fear of their newly realized nakedness. All of us have heard his accusations in our ears, in our minds, in our hearts. We hear the Accuser as soon as we give in to his temptation. After we take his bait, he blows the whistle and calls attention to our failure. The real tragedy is that we run and hide from God, the only one who removes our shame.

Have you ever seen stories on the news about criminals caught through undercover sting operations? I cannot help but feel a bit of pity for the perpetrators, whether they get caught trying to steal a bait car or are arrested soliciting an undercover cop they believed to be a prostitute. It's the same trick the Enemy uses. He plays nice as the tempter, then switches roles to the Accuser and blares the sirens of condemnation.

Eyes On Each Other - With our failure exposed, it's all too easy to look for fault elsewhere. Adam found fault in Eve for giving him the fruit, and in God for giving him Eve, all the while overlooking or minimizing his own culpability. I can't imagine what it must have felt like for Eve, after the heart-rending turn of events that day, to witness Adam selfishly distance himself from her. The consequences of taking our eyes from the Lord result in broken relationships between one another. Our sense of family and community becomes unsettled as we forsake our relational commitments for an "every man for himself" mentality. Self-preservation becomes our top priority. We don't look at the faults or needs of our fellow man with compassion; rather we shrug and say, "It's not my problem," and plod along in isolation from one another. This way of thinking amplifies the heaviness of spiritual death in our fractured fellowship between each other, and once again we feel alone. It is not good for man to be alone, our Creator said.

Fix Your Eyes

It is the oldest trick in the book, and it's used on us all of the time. We are persuaded to take our eyes off the holy, life-transforming image of God and turn them elsewhere, and without fail, the trouble begins. This is the history we keep repeating.

If we take the time to identify the deceptive voice and his motive behind tempting us, it's easy to distinguish the tone and know it is not the voice of Jesus. But more often than not we don't take the time, so quickly is our attention drawn to the object of our temptation. Sometimes we recognize the tempter but try to rebuff the temptation by reciting a law. Lies cloud our minds and we start to question God's motives in warning us about this temptation. We wonder if He's withholding good from us, as a child wonders what fun he's missing when a parent forbids him from sticking a fork in the toaster. Again, we stand in the midst of God's complete and life-giving provision and crave the fruit that brings death. We can naturally respond in two ways: 1) submit to sin, or 2) submit to law. With both options, the result is the same: slavery and death. There is but one way to supernaturally respond. Submit to the Spirit. The result is life.

So here we are in the aftermath. Those born of Adam (all of us) are born spiritually dead, disconnected from the loving Father. We are born without dominion, subjugated to sin. But those who have been made alive in Christ have been adopted into the family of God, bestowed with the riches of heaven and the declaration of new creation. If we do not fix our eyes on Jesus, the death that lurks in our mortal flesh seeps into our vision and blurs the Good News of new creation, convincing us that nothing's really changed other than our eternal destination. The Accuser starts whispering again, persuading our eyes to look elsewhere, and we try in vain to be our own solution. And so the problems continue.

The Distant Bride

"Who is this man, and what does he see in me?"

She never thought she would find love like this. This kind of love was out of her league. She had made more than her share of mistakes and always believed she would have to settle for less. The lovers she had known before had reinforced her belief that she was of low value, pitiful, fit only to be used, abused, and discarded. And yet, here she was, marrying a truly good man who supremely loved her with no contempt for her past. He gazed at her as though she were the most lovely and perfect bride who had ever walked the aisle. Any anxiety, doubts, or nagging thoughts of unworthiness disappeared when she looked into his eyes. All she saw was love, tenderness, acceptance, and devotion.

As the time came for them to consummate the marriage in the wedding chamber, he protested when she left his arms to become more "presentable." He desired her to remain by his side, but she insisted on one more reassuring glance in the mirror. Behind the closed bathroom door, she was horrified at her reflection. The harsh florescent light cast a squalid tint, intensifying the wrinkles on her face and revealing the dark circles beneath her eyes. She suppressed her welling panic and reached for her makeup. She knew how to fix this, she told herself, but the more makeup she applied, the more ghoulish her visage became. She washed her face to start again, and anxious, painful scrubbing produced sore, blotchy cheeks. Again she applied makeup, again she saw unpleasant results, and the panic returned. No amount of effort or covering up could overcome the ugliness the light revealed in that hideous mirror, and now black tears streaked down her marred and broken face.

"He won't want you now," the mirror told her. "You're not good enough for him."

She could not let him see her in such a state. She needed to fix this. Shrouding her face with a bath towel and fumbling for her coat and shoes, she left her heartsick groom behind. She ran out into the cold darkness, vowing not to return to him until she found a way to make herself beautiful again.

***

It is true; we are our own worst critics. We know the depths of our flaws, failures and depravity like the warts on our hands. We allow into our hearts the criticisms of others and mostly filter out the compliments and encouragement. Deep down we know that our critics don't even know how bad we are. It is far easier to believe the lies of the Enemy because we are surrounded by a fallen world full of discouragement. Those who buy into the Devil's lies surround us. We're all drinking from the same poisoned well. The words of love and affirmation from our bridegroom are too rich for us to accept, too good to be true. If we do believe His affirming words, we often believe His affirmation is connected to our piety and performance. Often we resort to an external code to measure internal progress. We put our eyes back on the command. Our intentions are good in that we are trying to please the Lord, but the fact remains that putting our eyes on the command either ensnares us in deception, sin, or the pride of personal achievement.

The Shame and Blame Game

The woman looking in the mirror on her wedding night is a picture of us judging ourselves by the standards we value. That is what we do with our knowledge of good and evil. We judge. We look in the mirror of the command to see if we look okay, or at least that we look better than those around us. The first judgment Adam and Eve made after eating the forbidden fruit was that it was shameful to be naked. They covered themselves with fig leaves and hid from God because of the shame they felt, not only in their nakedness, but also in knowing that they had done what God warned them to avoid.

When God came calling and found them hiding, He asked an interesting question. "Who told you that you were naked?" They had, of course, been without clothing all along, but they had not felt uncovered, unprotected, or vulnerable prior to eating the forbidden fruit. Adam responded to God's question defensively, and blamed both Eve and God in one statement.

"The woman that *You* gave me gave the fruit to me, and I ate." Adam, with his newfound knowledge of good and evil, tried to shirk responsibility for his own disobedience and even tried to pin the blame, out of all parties involved, on God! Eve got in on the act when it was her turn to give an account and pointed her finger at the serpent.

Again, these are the results of putting our eyes on each other. When our guilt or shame is exposed, it is our primary response to deflect and divert attention away from ourselves and cast blame elsewhere. In most cases we find that however horrible our transgression, there is usually someone doing a lot worse. "Now hold on," we protest. "What about THAT guy?!" Our pointing fingers trigger a domino effect of blame (which ultimately falls back to Adam and Eve).

I have discovered in my own life a link between feeling

judged and being judgmental of others. It's a condition of our fallen nature. Simply put, if you feel judged, you will judge. Say I were to come up to you and say, "Are you seriously wearing that outfit in public?" The first thing you will do is examine your own outfit, justify it, then shift your attention to my outfit, looking for fault in my clothing choices. You may be too polite to respond with criticism, but your judgmental side will most certainly get stirred up. Whether you voice it or keep it to yourself, you will return a judgment to the party who just passed judgment on you.

I grew up watching the Dallas Cowboys with my dad. As a lifelong fan of Cowboys football, I take a lot of flak (if you're not familiar with American professional football, there seems to be a disproportionate amount of vitriol aimed at the Cowboys, which I reason is due to jealousy at their successes, though other fans says it's because their fans are so annoying, but I don't know what they're talking about). Whenever someone teases me about cheering for the Cowboys, I always ask, "Who's your team?" Then I find ways to chide them in kind. Returning insult is not difficult, since only one NFL team has more Super Bowl victories to their credit than the Cowboys. If you don't know who that team is, you can look them up (rivalry prevents me from naming them). Sometimes folks respond with, "I don't have a team," at which point I condescendingly dismiss them and no longer give credence to their criticisms, believing that if they don't know what it's like to endure scorn for supporting a team, they have no room to criticize. Look at that, even writing about this topic stirs up my judgmental side!

These examples, petty and unimportant as they may be, really illuminate our tendency as humans to compare ourselves to one another to defend or improve our self-worth. We pass judgment using a set of criteria (the amount of championship titles your team has, performance of your quarterback in the playoffs, where your fans fall on the spectrum of obnoxiousness), which are often subjective. Sadly, Christians all too often make subjective and fleshly judgments about others, and not necessarily from a defensive standpoint. If we feel proud of our piety and ability to live up to the standard of our choosing, we go on the offensive and look for fault in others. Not even our own brothers and sisters are immune from the sentences we pass. In fact, we often judge them more harshly than we judge the world, since after all, they should know better (or so we think)! We judge under the banners of accountability or concern, but the standards we use to judge are inherently performance-based and Old Covenant in nature (as we shall examine in the next chapter). And that's not the only problem with being judgmental.

The Trouble with Judging

In college I learned of a psychological process humans constantly engage in called "uncertainty reduction." Any time we are uncertain about something or someone, we immediately set out to get answers or pick up clues about how to proceed. If we smell smoke, we try to find the fire. If we are riding the city bus and a man in a gorilla costume sits in the seat next to us, we need to figure out what is going on and if said gorilla is a threat to our safety, comfort, and/or dignity. We observe, we ask questions, and we most often arrive at instinctive and poorly researched conclusions. The result is we end up making a lot of assumptions about people based on our preconceived ideas. Again, speaking as a Dallas Cowboys fan, I have a stereotypical view that fans of our rival Philadelphia Eagles are lowbrow thugs. I know, of course, this is unfair and simply not true. Only most of them are lowbrow thugs (just teasing, Eagles fans, I have nothing but brotherly love for you).

It's a fine mess we're in. We judge others when their sin exceeds our own (by whatever standard we use to determine which sins are worse than others), and relegate those people to an inferior level beneath us. When we compare ourselves to someone we perceive to be doing better than us, we deal instead with the heaviness of our own inadequacy as we prop them up on a pedestal. The promotions or demotions we give others are determined from fluid standards of social acceptability and personal permissibility. As mere humans we form cliques, groups, or tribes with others who share our particular standards and definitions of right and wrong, good and evil, then we waste an ungodly amount of energy defending our standards and starting ideological wars with those who subscribe to a different viewpoint. These wars are fought with the carnal and polemical weapons of hate, shame, scorn, anger, and wrath.

From a human standpoint, I see the benefit of uncertainty reduction, but more clearly I regard the admonition of the Apostle Paul in 2 Corinthians 5:16 to no longer evaluate people from a human point of view. Among the glories of new creation is that Jesus has instituted a new order, free from fleshly distinctions and the wisdom of man, an order based completely on the wisdom of God and a new way of relating to Him and one another. In new creation life, we are not only transformed and invited to participate, we are revealed to be vital in God's plan to redeem creation as ministers of reconciliation. We do make judgments, but not merely as humans. Paul says in 1 Corinthians 2 we judge as the "spiritual man," gifted with the mind of Christ and the Holy Spirit, making judgments of all things but being judged by no one. A key distinction of these new creation judgments is they do not result in death and destruction. Sin, through the law, already accomplished that. Our judgments result in life and restoration. When we put our eyes on others with the vision of the Holy Spirit, we see their need for rescue and redemption.

Shortcomings of Right-or-Wrong Thinking

We need a new way of thinking, one that the Holy Spirit offers to us. We need to renew our minds to God's truth. The old way of thinking does not empower us to overcome the sin that so easily entangles us. Too often when people examine the temptations they habitually submit to, they say, "I know I shouldn't do this because it's wrong." My heart breaks when I hear that sentiment because it misses the point of God's life-giving ordinances. When those same people are honest, they will admit that they briefly feel better when they give in to temptation because the vice in question makes them temporarily forget their sorrow, pain, or emptiness. Of course, they find the emptiness remains and inevitably deepens as soon as the temporary pleasure subsides. They are trapped in a cycle of sin, guilt, shame, and remorse and for many, the only thing that brings temporary relief is to return to sin, the very thing that keeps them enslaved.

Please hear me carefully in a point I will make in different ways throughout this book; *choosing certain behaviors or patterns because you think they are right while avoiding other behaviors or patterns because you think they are wrong is not adequate motivation in the long run to beat temptation.* As I see it, the problems with right-or-wrong thinking, also called legalism, are three-fold.

To start, legalism has its foundation in an Old Covenant reliance on willpower and human effort to avoid the punishing consequences of law breaking and to receive the rewards and acceptance bestowed upon law-abiders. But willpower only gets you so far. If you have weak willpower, your failure leads you into a place of despair. If you have strong willpower, your success leads you into a place of pride or confidence in the flesh and keeps you in a pattern of self-reliance. We see this illustrated in Jesus' parable of the Pharisee and the tax collector

(Luke 18). The Pharisee, full of pride and self-reliance, did not recognize his own spiritual bankruptcy. The tax collector, in self-contempt and despair, felt the weight of his failures and clearly saw his need for God. Jesus concluded the parable by saying the tax collector's prayer was heard by God, but we see the solution to both men's problems was neither in self-reliance nor self-condemnation. The solution, Jesus knew as he told the story, would come through the cross and the empty tomb.

Secondly, the Bible speaks in Judges and Proverbs of man doing what is right in his own eyes. Most people are convinced that they are right in their thinking, and people who differ or disagree are obviously wrong. Because of that, you would be hard-pressed to show me a standard of right and wrong that is universally accepted. You may argue and say the world may not agree on a moral code, but Christians surely do, or at least they had better. But we know all too well that Christians are divided on a variety of doctrinal issues, and that church denominations have historically been birthed out of fiercely contested idealistic differences. It's easy to dismiss each other's distinctions of right and wrong as mere opinions. The spirit of this day and age increasingly attempts to discredit traditionally held values by challenging definitions and interpretations, all the while marginalizing those whose lives are Divinely governed. But our response cannot be "I'm right, you're wrong." That isn't the Good News, friends. We won't gain ground in the face of this adversity by focusing on finding fault with others. We will gain ground by the Spirit of God, by the wisdom of God, and by the weapons of the Spirit.

The third error of legalism is that it narrowly focuses on the categories of right and wrong, good and evil, without examining the intent and heart of the command. It only sees the prohibition of the command instead of the protection offered by it. Striving to avoid poor choices simply because "God says it's wrong" or "the Bible says it's wrong" paints God as a capricious and micromanaging lawgiver but completely overlooks His heart to protect us from the detrimental consequences of our thoughts, words, and actions. God did not say, "Thou shalt not kill" simply because killing is wrong, but because, among other things, it extinguishes the life of another and burdens the killer with a heavy, lifelong guilt. God did not say, "Thou shalt not commit adultery" simply because it's wrong, but because, among other reasons, it shows dishonor and breaks a precious covenant trust with your spouse, and because it's destructive to all families involved.

Not Command but New Creation

The legalistic approach looks to the command as an external motivator to produce internal change. It does not change our hearts, for indeed it cannot. Paul says in Romans 7 that the law is spiritual, but when we apply it to unregenerate flesh in hopes to attain fellowship and favor with God, we only discover the depth of our fleshly depravity. In fact, Paul explains the law incites rebellion in our flesh, even when our minds recognize it to be good and holy. No wonder Paul exclaimed, "Wretched man that I am! Who will deliver me from this body of death?" We did not have to wait long for his liberating answer in Romans 8:2, "For the law of the Spirit of life has set you free in Christ Jesus from the law of sin and death."

In Galatians 5:6, Paul spoke of the solution and spoke against Old Covenant distinctions of right and wrong. "For in Christ Jesus neither circumcision or uncircumcision counts for anything, but faith working through love." The letter to the Galatians strongly opposed those trying to add to Christ's completely sufficient sacrifice, as some were persuading new followers of Jesus that they still must obey precepts of the Old Covenant, especially circumcision, in order to have fellowship with God. Paul reasserted his precept in Galatians 6 saying the only thing that counted was new creation. After the resurrection, ascension, and glorification of Jesus, the Apostle Paul said in 2 Corinthians 5, "We used to look at Jesus according to the flesh, but we do so no longer," and further that we no longer regard or recognize people according to human standards. Then Paul writes some of the most beloved words in scripture, "Therefore, if anyone is in Christ, he is new creation. The old has passed away; behold, the new has come."

Let those words sink in. We no longer look at people with human standards. We no longer arrive at conclusions with the mind of man. Now that we are in Christ, we live in new creation. The old distinctions have disappeared. We arrive at conclusions now with the mind of Christ that has been gifted to us through the indwelling of the Spirit of Jesus. The old has passed away and the new has come. There is neither Jew nor Greek. There is neither slave nor free. There is neither male nor female. Those who are in Christ are one in Christ. Those who are not in Christ need our ministry of reconciliation, as Christ desires all to experience new life in Him.

Free from Judgment

In Christ, you are free from being judged by worldly standards. Does this mean people will no longer pass judgment on you? No, sorry, it doesn't mean that. You will be opposed and even persecuted for being a Kingdom ambassador. But when you are sheltered in the mighty fortress of Christ, those judgments lose their power over you. The condemnation loses its sting. If you are in Christ, the Accuser's pronouncements against you are baseless and hollow. According to Colossians 2, the legal code used to harass and condemn you was nailed to the cross with Jesus. Not only are you free from condemnation; *you are free from condemning others.* Your knowledge of good and evil has been upgraded to Holy Spirit revelation through the mind of Christ and you no longer need to play "gotcha" when you catch someone in sin. You are free, praise God, from making insufficient and ineffective judgments against others using worldly standards. You are free to love those the legal code would cause you to despise, and only that love, the divine love of God birthed in the hearts of those who have been forgiven much, has the power to break shackles off the captives and bring them into liberty.

Can I take this opportunity to remind us all of Paul's words in Ephesians 6 that our struggle is not against flesh and blood? Let me elaborate. Our struggle is not against Pharisees. Our struggle is not against denominations whose doctrines vary from ours. Our struggle is not against atheists. Our struggle is not against neo-Nazis. Our struggle is not against Muslim extremists. Our struggle is not against terrorists. Our struggle is not against Democrats. Our struggle is not against Republicans. Our struggle is not against homosexuals, heterosexuals, transsexuals, gun-rights activists, anti-gun activists, pro-lifers, pro-choicers, drunkards, tea-totallers, Tea Partiers, oil barons, Wall Street tycoons, bank executives, warmongers, pacifists, evolutionists, creationists, transcendentalists, existentialists, naturalists, industrialists, journalists, or legalists. Our struggle is against the spiritual forces of evil in heavenly places: the enemy who conspires to keep us all in brokenness.

We are not called to war against the people Jesus died to save. Ministers of reconciliation do not shame people into the Kingdom of God. We do not mock or cajole them, even when they mock and cajole our faith. We do not smirk and gloat at the thought of them facing eternal separation from God. We do not satisfy our fleshly thirst for vengeance by reminding ourselves we will have the last laugh. No, rather we have the same mind of Jesus, who was God in His very nature but did not demand rights as God (and what rights do we demand that don't even come close to that?). He humbled himself, obeyed His Father (and our Father), suffered at the hands of the world to the point of death, and forgave them in the final moments of His life. Then the Spirit of God raised Him from the dead, and Jesus later breathed that Spirit into us. With that Spirit, we walk out our commission to announce the Gospel of grace to the world. We pause and remember in the heat of division and strife with our fellow man the graciousness shown to us while we were broken, in darkness, and hostile to God, and recall how He healed us and changed us through the love of Jesus. We win the unbeliever through imploring them to be reconciled to the Father. We win them through unflinching, unconditional love. The Spirit of the Lord God is upon us, yes, even you and me, to preach Good News to the poor, to bind up the broken-hearted, to proclaim liberty to the captives, to open the eyes of the blind, to free the oppressed, and to declare the time of God's favor and blessing!

Out of Eden

The everlasting, unchanging God is the God of love and grace. He did not leave Adam and Eve in their shame, nor did He leave them in the garden where they might eat of the Tree of Life and continue immortally in their sinful condition. He did not leave them clothed in man-made fig-leaf fashions from their "Fall" collection. He provided covering for them, at the cost of the shed blood of an innocent animal. He did not turn His back on them, but time and again appealed in love and mercy to the sons of man to be reconciled.

But man's heart was set on evil, a penalty of Adam and Eve's disobedience. Man had tunnel vision on doing what was right in his own eyes, the same easily deceived eyes that judged the poisonous fruit to be good.

Adam and Eve passed on the knowledge of good and evil to all their descendants, including you and me, of course. God prophesied that the Savior, the seed of the woman, would one day come to crush the head of the serpent. As God covered the shame of Adam and Eve with the skin of a sacrificial animal, our shame would be covered by Jesus, the Lamb of God.

But before Jesus would come, Moses came. And went.

Chapter 3
MOSES DIDN'T GET US HERE

"The law came through Moses," the Apostle John declares in the opening chapter of his gospel, "but grace and truth came through Jesus Christ." Moses, without a doubt, had an essential role to play in the grand story of God's covenant. He was raised up at a crucial time in the history of Israel to liberate the people of Abraham, Isaac, and Jacob from their slavery in Egypt. God sent Moses in response to the cries of His children as they languished in bondage. God used Moses to partially fulfill the covenant with Abraham that his descendants would multiply, inhabit a promised land, and one day release blessing to all the nations of the earth.

I honor Moses for his faithfulness and friendship to God, but I do not confuse him for the one who brought salvation to the ends of the earth. That accomplishment and honor solely belongs to Jesus. Sadly, many people of faith have granted Moses equal or nearly equal status with Jesus. Would-be followers of Jesus have been convinced that after salvation, the way to stay in favor with God is by sticking to pertinent bits of the Old Covenant or some modified version of a moral code. This idea of humans attaining a standard worthy of fellowship and favor with God, of living up to an ideal image, is ancient and is found in many world religions. A quick survey of religions that have existed for millennia will reveal that they all contain an ethical standard or a checklist of sorts for achieving the approval of the Almighty. I contend that this was not the point in the giving of the Old Covenant, and it is certainly not the point of following Jesus.

It is important for me to distinguish that the message of grace has become more accepted in modern Christianity, and for that I rejoice. There is a firm understanding that we are saved by grace through faith and not by works, as Ephesians 2:8-9 states. However, there remains a prevailing mindset in much of the church, as I discussed in my own story earlier, that after receiving the saving grace of Jesus, it is now among our chief purposes to live holy and righteous lives, and the way to achieve that is by following an external code that governs our behavior. This is where Moses commonly gets reintroduced into our thinking. We are pointed to the Ten Commandments and other tenets of the Mosaic covenant, and we set out to craft an updated code that also includes "New Testament Law" from the teachings of Jesus and the apostles.

I spent too much of my life, as do many Christians, believing that adherence to such a code of morality was the essence of following Jesus. My religious practices consisted of doing right and avoiding wrong. Do your best and clean up your mess. I got my spiritual "to do" list from a number of Bible sources; the ten commandments, the books of the law, the Proverbs, the teachings of Jesus, the writings of Paul, Peter, James, and John. I had extra-biblical motivators for holiness as well. Sermons, Sunday School lessons, Christian tracts, t-shirts, bumper stickers, hymns, choruses, and songs on Christian radio. From this patchwork quilt of do-it-yourself morality, I learned and kept track of how a "good" Christian was supposed to act, and what a "strong" Christian looked like. What I didn't realize is I had fallen for the scheme of the Enemy to take my eyes off Jesus and put my eyes on the command. You'll recall that led me to trouble (I also put my eyes on others to gauge my progress in comparison to theirs). When I finally realized that Moses was in fact pointing us to salvation through Jesus, my appreciation and understanding of Moses and his role grew immensely.

Moses and Jesus

Moses was indeed a type of Christ. In studying the Exodus account and the wilderness journey, we see shadows of the Messiah. Years ago, after studying the striking similarities and history-changing differences between Moses and Jesus, I wrote a song called "Moses Didn't Get Us Here." May the Lord bless you with understanding as you read these lyrics:

Verse 1
He started out as royalty, a scepter in his hand
But a shepherd's staff soon took its place
He was sent out to free the slaves held in a foreign land
And the glory of the Lord shone on his face

Called to climb a hillside from a crowd and all alone
There to write down words the Lord would say
A covenant God offered, firmly carved in stone
The people would be blessed if they obey

He died upon a mountain, he was laid to rest by God
And in his grave his mortal bones remain .
God raised up a new leader to take His people to the land
A place of rest that they must first obtain

Verse 2
He started out as royalty, a scepter in His hand
But a shepherd's staff soon took its place
He was sent out to free the slaves held in a foreign land
And through this One the Lord revealed His grace

49

Called to climb a hillside, in a crowd but all alone
He hung accursed, His lost sheep to retrieve
A covenant God offered, carved in flesh and bone
The people will be blessed if they believe.

He died upon a mountain, He was laid to rest by man
In a borrowed grave, He was not there to stay
God raised Him on the third day to take His people to the land
The end of works, this endless Sabbath day

Verse 3
Still somehow we try to keep the law that brings us death
And every time we try to stand, we fall
Moses' life ended in death, Jesus' death ended in life
And now He lives to bring new life to all

When you breathe the breath of freedom,
When the veil has been torn down
When you know the love of Christ has drawn you near
When you stand before your Father
and grace and peace abound
Then you know that Moses did not get us here
You know that Moses did not get us here
You know that Moses did not get us here

Woeful in the Wilderness?

The story of Moses has long intrigued me because of what I perceived as a heartbreaking ending. I always felt like Moses got a raw deal. He made some mistakes in his younger years, fled the scene of a murder he committed, and then paid his dues for four decades on the backside of the desert, tending sheep. God used him mightily to deliver the Hebrews from Egypt, and he steadfastly sought the face of the Lord, even when those in his care grumbled and complained and time after time showed a complete lack of faith in Moses and God. Moses spoke face to face with God, as with a friend. Moses received God's Law on tablets of stone and delivered its words to the nation. Moses persuaded the Lord to stay His hand when God resolved to wipe his rebellious people out. Moses judged with wisdom.

Then came a fateful, seemingly small blunder. The people complained about a lack of water and God told Moses to speak to the rock in order to receive water. Once before, following God's instructions at Horeb, Moses struck the rock that provided water for the people. But the water-providing rock at Kadesh, foreshadowing the provision of living water to come from the Rock of Ages, had been struck once and now only needed speaking to. Moses was angry at the stubbornness and hard-hearted ways of the people, so he struck the rock. God honored his prophet and produced water, but the consequences for Moses were severe, consequences he would take to the grave. He would not take his people into the Promised Land, nor would he enter it himself. It would fall to Joshua to finish the task and lead the people into Canaan. God would show the land to Moses from a distance, and then God would lay Moses to rest.

Moses saw the Promised Land from the top of Mount Pisgah, according to Deuteronomy 34, and then he died, though his vision had not dimmed and his strength had not failed. God buried him, and to this day no one knows the location of his grave.

Perhaps you share my heartbreak. How could God give His people so many second chances at the behest of Moses, and yet forbid Moses, the one He spoke face to face with as to a friend, from leading the people into their destiny? One moment of anger directed at the people with whom God had been plenty angry, and Moses was disqualified from finishing the quest to which he had devoted so much of his life. It did not seem fair.

Then I began to find references to this story elsewhere in scripture. I read in John 1 about the law coming through Moses, but grace and truth coming through Jesus Christ. I saw in Hebrews 4 that the Promised Land represented a rest from works of the law. I studied the parable of the rich man in torment imploring Abraham to send warning messengers to his brothers, and heard Abraham's response, "They have Moses and the prophets. Let them listen to them." And then, in a passage of New Covenant revelation, I saw an iconic cast of characters standing atop the Mount of Transfiguration. I saw Moses as the Law. I saw Elijah as the Prophets. I saw Jesus, Yeshua, the one foretold and foreshadowed. And I heard the voice of the Father saying, "This is my beloved Son. Listen to *Him*." When the dazzling glory of the Lord faded, there alone stood Jesus. No Elijah, for the One the prophets spoke of had arrived. No Moses, for the law had served its purpose in revealing the need for a Savior, and as Hebrews 8:13 says, was ripe for disappearance.

The book of Hebrews also talks of the elements of the Old Covenant being merely types and shadows of heavenly reality. The tabernacle, and later the temple, were representations of the spiritual dwelling place of God, though His Shekinah glory dwelled there. The blood of bulls and goats shed on the day of atonement was a shadow of the blood of Jesus being offered in the true Holy of Holies, God's heavenly dwelling. If Moses represents the law and the Promised Land represents rest from works of the law, then God's judgment against Moses no longer seems cruel and arbitrary but completely necessary! Can following the law lead to a rest from works of the law? Paul answers this in Romans 3:20, "For by works of the law no human being will be justified in His sight, since through the law comes knowledge of sin." The more you try to live by the law, the more the law finds you guilty and condemns you. The more you try, the more you fail, and the harder your heart of stone becomes. Moses could not lead the people into a place of rest because the covenant he represented could not either!

A Covenant Primer

One of the blessings of belonging to New Life City is hearing rich preaching and instruction from Pastor Alan Hawkins, especially on the subject of covenant. The majority of what I know about covenant comes from his teaching. While there are great books yet to be written about what he knows, I will give you some basics.

A covenant is a mutually beneficial bond between two parties. Unlike a contract that protects the parties from each other should one fail to uphold the terms of the agreement, a covenant seeks the blessing and provision of both parties by one another (think of a marriage covenant in which the husband and wife both pledge to make each other's needs as important as their own). In biblical covenants, there are common markers such as the giving of gifts and the shedding of blood, and there are many examples of covenant throughout the scriptures. While the covenant with Moses (commonly referred to as the Old Covenant) is perhaps the most well known from the days before Jesus ratified the New Covenant through the shedding of His own blood, a greater covenant preceded it. I speak of the covenant God made with Abram (as told in Genesis 12 and 15).

In response to Abram's faith to leave his home and go where God led, God promised Abram his name would be great, his descendants would outnumber the stars in the sky and the sands on the seashore, and that all the world would be blessed through his offspring. This was a prophecy of the coming Messiah who would defeat sin and death and bring all who believed in Him into the family of God. God also told Abram that one day his offspring would be captives in Egypt for

400 years, but God would deliver them and give them the land promised to Abram.

400 years after Jacob and his family settled in Egypt, God gave the Old Covenant to the Israelites through Moses at Mount Sinai. It was given as a temporary covenant until the Messiah's arrival. It was given to protect and govern the people of God, but it could only do so if the people obeyed the law. The law was good, just, and perfect, but of course, the people were not. The sinful nature inherited from Adam kept interfering with their ability to uphold the law. The result again and again was death.

The Letter Kills

Paul boldly says in 2 Corinthians 3:6 that the letter kills, but the Spirit gives life. For genuine change to occur, it has to happen in our hearts and minds and be empowered by the Holy Spirit or it will not last. Only a change of heart produces lasting, internal *and* external results. Remember that one of the chief problems we have with the letter of the law is that it invariably stirs up our sinful nature (that's part of its design). Paul even says in Romans 5:20 that the law was added to increase the trespass (and remove all doubt that we need salvation). Understand when I speak of the letter of the law I am not just talking about the Mosaic Law of the Old Covenant (a covenant, it should be noted, that was never given to us living today). I am not just talking about all the New Testament commands and instructions some people think have been added to the list of Old Covenant. Living by the letter of the law means following codes, regulations, rules, restrictions, commands, ordinances, "ought to's and shoulds" in order to stay in favor with God. Living by the letter of the law means shifting the focus from "done" to "do," from provision to prohibition. Living by the letter of the law puts our eyes on the command, which puts our eyes on temptation. It makes us question God and His ordinance, stirs up our sinful nature, and provides the opportunity to rebel.

DO NOT SKIP AHEAD TO READ THE LAST PAGE OF THIS BOOK!

Do you see what I just did? I introduced a law. Arbitrary? Yes. Inconsequential? Absolutely. But I can typically predict one of three responses: 1) You law-abiders did not, and would not dream of skipping ahead to read the last page, 2) Those of you who are outlaws skipped ahead, because I'm not the boss of you, and no one tells you what to do, or 3) You know me and have heard me teach this lesson before, and there's no way you are falling for that trick again. For the sake of my law-abiding crowd, I give you permission to read the last page of the book if you so desire.

In 2 Corinthians 3, Paul makes an amazing comparison of the Old and New Covenants, also referring to them respectively as the ministry of death and the ministry of the Spirit, the ministry of condemnation and the ministry of righteousness, and the covenant of ending glory and the covenant of surpassing and permanent glory. He discusses the effects of both covenants being read. Let us revisit this glorious comparison.

When Moses came down from Mount Sinai with the commandments on tablets of stone, his face shone with the glory he encountered in the presence of the Lord. So bright was his countenance and so deep was the Israelites' fear that they could not gaze upon it. Moses covered up with a veil, but not only because of the brightness. According to Paul, the veil was there because the glory was fading and Moses did not want the Israelites to see it diminish. He wished for the Israelites to remain in a state of awe and respect for the Covenant.

Paul further states that "to this day" a veil remains on the hearts of the hearer when the Old Covenant is read. Of course, Paul's day is long since gone, but I believe those words still ring true to *this* day. The Hebrews heard the words of the Old Covenant and initially reacted with an awe that produced adherence and submission, but in just a short time their hearts were hardened as they fashioned and worshipped a golden calf. Even those abiding by the law felt the condemnation and subsequent death that comes from the law.

And to *this* day, you can still feel that death, even though most of us do not feel compelled to abide by the tedious requirements of the Old Covenant (minus the big ones, of course). But we feel the effect of Paul's words, "the letter kills." Many times when you are instructed to abide by the letter of the law, you experience, even in small ways, the threat of condemnation.

I will highlight this point with one of my ministry experiences (the names and events have been changed to protect the innocent). I once worked at a church that operated a 24-hour prayer ministry. The church member in charge informed me I needed to pick a slot and help out. The concept was sound and birthed out of good intentions. I signed up to pray once weekly during a fixed, one-hour slot. The person praying in the time slot before would call at the end of his hour to remind me it was my turn, just to ensure there were no gaps in the prayer coverage. I would then dial an automated phone line through which people would record voice messages detailing their requests. I would write down the requests, pray for the remainder of my hour, and then call the person signed up for the next hour. It was a great idea with pure motives behind it, and who could say no to prayer ministry?

The first week I was full of zeal. I called to retrieve messages and jot down notes. *Pray for Jane's sister who has pneumonia. Pray that Larry can find a wife. Pray for Bobbi's cat Sparkles who has been missing for over two days and she's very worried.* I dutifully prayed, passed the baton, and got on with my week.

The second week my enthusiasm had slightly waned, but I had made a commitment and I was not going to allow gaps in prayer coverage. I called to retrieve messages and jot down notes. *Jane's sister got over pneumonia but her bunions are killing her. Larry really needs a wife. Bobbi's cat Sparkles has been missing for over a week. Fliers with Sparkles' picture have been distributed through the neighborhood but no luck yet.* I soldiered through and prayed for most of my hour, calling my replacement just a little bit earlier than usual.

By week three I was starting to feel the burden of my task, and honestly feeling some resentment toward my indefinite obligation. While I struggled to find motivation to pray, I was driven forward by curiosity to hear updates. *Jane's sister is seeing a podiatrist next week, so pray for that to go well. Larry really, REALLY needs a wife. Bobbi has not seen her cat in two weeks. Also, there's a strange smell coming from under the front porch.*

The letter kills. The obligation of a decree has the tendency to drain the life out of a sound idea. Think about the extremely low success rates we have at keeping our New Year's resolutions. We want to see change in our lives, we aspire to accomplish something good and worthwhile, therefore we set goals for ourselves to achieve those things. There is nothing wrong with our intent, and often it is the Holy Spirit prompting this change, but again, when we apply external motivators in hopes to see internal change, we struggle to achieve our goal and retain the desired results. As we realize our old nature is too strong to overcome with resolutions and willpower, we become despondent and feel the guilt and disappointment of our failures. We struggle to believe we can ever change or achieve anything worthwhile. We are certain that we're exhausting the grace of God. We feel Paul's struggle in Romans

7 and cry out, "Who can deliver me from this body of death?" We see ourselves as dead and buried with the tablets of law as our tombstones. And there the law accomplishes its purpose, condemning us to death and showing us again our need for Jesus, our savior and deliverer.

What the Law Does and Does Not Do

Due to stricter environmental laws to combat the effects of pollution, vehicles in America must have periodic emissions testing to ensure the levels of pollutants do not exceed government standards. Vehicles that exceed the standards must be repaired or kept off the road.

Years ago, I acquired a 1979 Ford pickup from my father-in-law for a great price. It was an ugly monster. It was mostly dark brown, dented, scratched, and quite an eyesore. I loved it. After logging a few thousand miles, though, I noticed the truck was having exhaust trouble. Cars behind me in traffic were left in a half-mile haze of smoke, and when it was time to have my emissions tested, I was more than a little nervous.

I drove my truck into the single-vehicle testing booth where the attendant closed the booth doors and instructed me to rev up my engine. When I stepped on the gas pedal, my exhaust pipe belched not just a puff of smoke, but the pillar of cloud that led the Israelites through the wilderness by day! The attendant barely escaped with his life. Okay, I exaggerate, but my truck failed the test miserably. I was flummoxed. I asked the attendant what I should do. He shrugged and said, "Take it to a mechanic." The emissions test does not repair the problem. It only reveals it.

And so it was with the law. The law revealed transgression but offered no solution or salvation. The law revealed man's old nature to be corrupt to the core and only capable of sin. To make matters worse, the old nature was stained and sinful before the law was given, but when the law was revealed, it not only revealed humanity to be lawbreakers, but it aroused man's sinful passions, according to Paul in Romans 7. Sin took advantage of the tempting opportunity the law provided and put man to death by the law. Those outside of God's covenant who sinned apart from the law died apart from the law, Paul explains in Romans 2. It reminds me of the old "push the unsuspecting guy over your kneeling buddy" routine. The law was there like a consequential barrier, unflinching and unyielding, and temptation shoved man over, laughing as he fell. And there he laid, dead in trespasses and sins. The only hope of redemption was a new nature altogether, and a New Covenant.

Why Do We Try and Keep the Law?

There are some key clues in the garden of Eden that provide insight into our tendency to keep the letter of the law. The effect of eating the forbidden fruit was to give mankind the knowledge of good and evil. Along with that knowledge, however, came the reality that man's efforts to be good and avoid evil were confounded by his sinful nature. The realization of nakedness and the shame that accompanied it made man hide from God, the source of life. In the presence of God's goodness, Adam and Eve recognized their shortcomings and hid, even using fig leaves to cover their shame. As I see it, the first reason we try to keep the law is to somehow diminish the distance between God's goodness and our fallenness.

I believe a bigger reason for our legal striving is hardwired into the fallen nature. When God pronounced the changes following Adam and Eve's disobedience, notice what they had in common. Adam would toil and struggle to produce sustenance from the earth, and Eve would endure pain and difficulty in childbirth. They would have to work and suffer to sustain life. The second reason we try to keep the law is we believe anything worth having has to be worked for, fought for, or paid for.

That mindset is evident in the way we conduct ourselves today. We are reluctant to accept gifts and charity, prone to earn our way. Though I was once mystified by religions or practices that required severe penance and varying degrees of self-abuse or self-flagellation, I understand it now. Deep down, we've resigned ourselves to miserable suffering. We hope our scars will count for something. When called into account, we hope our deeds will weigh out in our favor. So we embrace our pain, even in defiance against the futility of existence.

Please hear me clearly. We were created to work. We were born with a need for significance and purpose. Adam named animals and tended the garden, co-laboring with the Lord, and it was a joy. Ecclesiastes 5:19 says enjoying your work is a gift from God. Above that, we as followers of Christ have the amazing privilege of working with God to spread the Good News of a new creation way of living. That's the purpose for which our strength is to be used. My warning here is against spending your God-given strength and energy trying to attain the blessings of new creation God has already given you through faith in Jesus, the riches of grace, salvation, healing, righteousness, justification, and sanctification. These are appropriated, not by works, but by faith in the death, burial, and resurrection of Jesus. Stop draining yourself of precious energy meant for the work of the Gospel and the rescue of others by striving for what's already yours!

Following Yeshua

Moses, on God's orders, gave the law to protect and govern Israel, and to preserve the bloodline from Abraham to Jesus. Jesus came in grace to open up the family to all who believe and receive Him. Moses could not lead the people into the Promised Land, as the law cannot lead us into a place of rest. The law, like Moses, had to be laid to rest by God, even though, like Moses, it still had vigor and its strength had not diminished. Jesus marched up a mountain, like Moses, to die. Nailed upon the cross with Jesus was the written code that legally condemned us as lawbreakers. God buried Moses, and only God could bury the law in the person of Jesus Christ who had fulfilled it. And in the grave the Old Covenant remains, with Hebrews 8:13 declaring it obsolete.

Who then will lead us into the place of rest? Yeshua will, of course. Joshua and Jesus both share the Hebrew name Yeshua (Salvation), and not coincidentally. You remember Joshua as Moses' servant who would remain in the Tent of Meeting with the presence of the Lord even after Moses would leave the tent (Exodus 33:11). You remember Joshua as a warrior who defeated the Amalekites while Moses stood on a hill holding up the staff of God and ensuring victory. You remember Joshua as Caleb's lone faithful companion among the twelve spies, ten of whom did not believe they could trust God and inhabit the land He promised them. And you remember Joshua as the successor of Moses. When Joshua led them to the Jordan River, as Moses had led them to the Red Sea, the people again crossed on dry ground behind the priests carrying the Ark of the Covenant, the throne of God's Spirit. The Red Sea was parted down the middle, while the flow of the Jordan River was interrupted upriver to provide a crossing. This verse, in my opinion, is particularly significant:

"The water from upstream stopped flowing. It piled up in a heap a great distance away, at a town called Adam." Joshua 3:16

You should know my mind works in such a way that I'm constantly searching for parallel meaning and analogies in scripture. There appears to be some strong symbolism in this passage that connects the leadership of Jesus to that of Joshua, even more so than Moses. Please allow me to explain, with the disclaimer that these are simply my conclusions, not necessarily Gospel truth.

Jesus is the only deliverer who can take us into a place of rest from works of the law, the glorious sabbath rest of the New Covenant. We passed from death into life, Ephesians 2 says, and the inherited sinful nature that coursed through our veins stopped flowing. The sinful flow from our forefathers, that threatened to wash us away like a river in flood, was piled up in a heap a great distance away from us, at Adam. The last Adam, the firstborn of new creation made this possible by His selfless, atoning sacrifice. We entered a new land by faith, led by the Holy Spirit as a new race to reclaim from the enemy territory promised to us. This land is a place of everlasting rest in the Father's love, a land full of grace and the blessings of God's abundant provision. And Moses didn't get us here.

In a beautiful and redemptive postscript to this story, Moses did eventually end up in the Promised Land, in the company of Jesus and Elijah on the mountaintop where Jesus was transfigured. And then, seeing Salvation in the flesh, the One whom they foreshadowed and prophesied, Moses and Elijah disappeared in the dazzling glory of the beloved Son of God.

Old Covenant Eulogy

Here lies Old Covenant. We call him "Old" but he wasn't the original covenant. He was good. Really good. He was virtuous, righteous, the very picture of morality. He served honorably as a judge his entire life. He came on the scene in a blaze of glory, but honestly, it was all downhill from there. Don't get me wrong, he maintained his righteousness until the very end, but he left a trail of condemnation everywhere he went.

He was an awe-inspiring character. People never felt

worthy in his presence. And there was this character that always lurked along behind Old Covenant. His name was Sin, and he was mainly an opportunist. He'd hear what Old Covenant said, then sneak over and present you with a tempting counter-argument, a dare to go against Old Covenant, all the while assuring you it was no big deal. But as soon as you fell for Sin's lies, Old Covenant would find you guilty of your transgressions and condemn you, then this other character named Consequences would show up. He was a real buzzkill.

Yeah, good Old Covenant. He was good, but he wasn't the best. Old Covenant was glorious, vital and healthy to the end. His strength had not diminished, and his vision had not faded. He was useful as a tutor who exasperated his pupils into the recognition that they needed a savior, but was unable to provide salvation. He could see the Promised Land from the mountaintop, but he couldn't lead people into it. In all his years as a judge, he found every single defendant guilty, all but One. As it turns out, the One found not guilty was sentenced to death anyway, but through that death He introduced us to the infinitely more glorious New Covenant.

Old Covenant is "survived" by those who want to see his legacy continued, people with veils on their hearts who just won't accept God's proclamation that Old Covenant is obsolete, and that the way into the presence of God is through faith in His resurrected Son, Jesus. Old Covenant's legacy is also proliferated by principalities, powers, and even religious institutions that wish to use Old Covenant as leverage, to control and exploit the guilt of those who don't know or can't believe Old Covenant has passed on, and to keep them caught in a cycle of self-reliance, temptation, and failure. In lieu of sympathy, God the Father has requested we send thanks and praise to Jesus Christ, and that we joyfully and gratefully celebrate our freedom in Him, trust Him with our lives, and walk in the resurrection power of His Spirit.

Time to Move On

There is something comfortable about knowing what's expected of you. There is a great elimination of uncertainty when your tasks are spelled out for you. It even feels good for our flesh to struggle and suffer a bit so we can boast that we pulled ourselves up by our own bootstraps. Again, that's the way of self-reliance, and that way does not lead to life. Please understand I'm not speaking against a heartfelt attempt to walk in a manner pleasing to the Lord. I'm not saying that grace turns a blind eye to destructive behavior and lawlessness. I'm not encouraging people to sow their wild oats with no regard for the unwanted yet inevitable harvest of consequences. I'm saying grace empowers you to walk according to a new and greater law: the law of the Spirit.

Following Jesus means walking in faith, living in vital union with Him, depending on Him for everything. Once the believing Israelites followed Yeshua into the Promised Land, they knew the giants were not going to leave easily, but they had confidence that God was fighting for them and leading the way.

Chapter 4
GRACE BY WHICH WE STAND

The covenant of Law served its purpose. It provided governance for the Israelites as they became a nation. It provided protection for God's people. It also condemned everyone living under it (just as those outside of the covenant were also condemned) and offered temporary atonement for sins committed. Finally, it brought forth the seed of the woman, the seed of Abraham, Jesus the Messiah, who brought salvation to all who would believe, both Jews and Gentiles.

Moses did his job and punched the clock. This New Covenant by which we now boldly approach the throne of God is one of grace, a gift provided to us through the faithfulness of Jesus. Grace is a divine attribute of the triune God, an aspect of His generous character and a facet of His nature that invites us to partake of that same nature. Grace provided for you what God required of you. Grace pulled you from the miry pit and put your feet on the Solid Rock. Grace met you on the road home at the end of your prodigal journey and wouldn't hear your excuses, joyfully choosing instead to clothe you in Christ's righteousness and throw a party for you. Grace killed the sinner who reigned in your body and brought to life your spirit, which now bears witness with the Spirit of God that you are indeed His child. Grace is how you stand and how you walk as God's child in the Promised Land. Grace has granted you access to the indwelling Holy Spirit, who now enables you to conquer giants and possess your inheritance.

Exodus Explained

While the exodus story chronicles God's people leaving Egypt, receiving the Old Covenant, and becoming a nation, it does much more than that: it richly foreshadows the New Covenant. The revelation of the Gospel in the wilderness journey has renewed my mind to the beauty of God's grace.

Again, in searching for the analogous, deeper meaning of Old Covenant passages, it's plain to see that the liberation of the Hebrew children from Egyptian slavery correlates to the rescue Jesus brought through our salvation. From my former, performance-based vantage point, I once saw crossing the Red Sea as Christian baptism, and I saw the wilderness wandering as the best we believers could expect on this side of eternity. My understanding was life would be a meager, joyless, mostly difficult existence with a bland menu until we died, at which point we would finally cross the Jordan and enter the promised land of eternity. But now, after understanding what I shared with you in the previous chapter, the Exodus events, viewed through New Covenant revelation, take their proper place.

Without a doubt, Jesus not only rescued us from the slavery of sin and death, just as Moses rescued the Hebrews from Egypt, but He so thoroughly defeated sin and overcame death that we no longer need to look over our shoulders to see if that old enemy is still in hot pursuit. The drowning of the Egyptian army in the Red Sea speaks of the finality of Christ's defeat of sin (which Hebrews 10 says He dealt with once and for all). Sin, like the aggressive Egyptian army, was wiped out, it's power neutralized. But you'll notice that even though the Egyptian army no longer held power over the Israelites, in times of grumbling they often spoke of returning to slavery. Don't we do the same thing? Even though we are free from the tyranny of sin, we still willingly long for and sometimes return to the place of our former captivity.

The wilderness journey, complete with hardship, trials, and tests of faith, is not a picture of new creation life but of life under the law. If you're a Christian trying to honor God through an Old Covenant mindset, I relate to your misery! The Exodus is a picture of following Moses, not following Jesus. Paul confirms this in 1 Corinthians 10:2 by saying the Israelites were "baptized into Moses in the cloud and in the sea" (though Paul states in the passage that they drank spiritual water from the rock that was Jesus). It was in the wilderness at Mount Sinai that the law was given by God through Moses. It was there that the people in terror begged Moses to keep God from speaking directly to them (a request God honored, speaking only through prophets until the New Covenant). It was there that the Lord dwelt as cloud and fire in the midst of the people, though He was not accessible to them. It was a place of restlessness and peril, of rebellion and death.

Most significantly, it was a place of unbelief. Time and again, the Israelites doubted the Lord. They grumbled and complained and reasoned that Moses had led them out of Egypt to die in the wilderness with parched throats and empty bellies. This after watching God manifest His glory through the ten plagues, through parting the waters at the Red Sea, and through utterly destroying Pharaoh and his army. When they were thirsty, the Lord quenched their thirst. When they were hungry, He provided manna. When they grew tired of manna, He sent quail. When their enemies opposed them, He fought for them. How did they respond to His graciousness? When He told the Israelites He was the Lord their God, they fashioned a golden calf to worship. When He spoke, they wanted Him silenced. And finally, upon arrival at the land God promised them, the people believed the faithless report from the ten spies who said they could not possess the land because the inhabitants were too strong to overcome. Even when Caleb told of the worth of the land and the strength of God, they refused to accept his report. What was behind their unbelief? Fear. Their fear of the enemy caused doubt. Fear that God would not do what He promised to do. Fear that God would not be there for them.

Time after time God had shown Himself faithful. Time after time He provided for their needs. Time after time He displayed His might and power on their behalf, and yet the Israelites feared the inhabitants of the land that only twelve of them had even seen. God's judgment came swiftly. All those over the age of 20 who refused to believe would die in the wilderness and never inhabit the Promised Land. Hebrews 3 talks of those who could not enter His rest because of unbelief as those who do not know the ways of the Lord and who always go astray in their hearts. I find this to be a sobering warning to those who claim to know God. These were chosen, covenant people who had been told the words of God and shown the ways of God, but when the test of faith came, they would not rely on God. Today, there are people who know of God and try to adhere to some semblance of morality, but will not trust God with their lives, their families, their relationships, their money, their sexual impulses, their career, their past, or their future.

But there is a better way through a better covenant with better promises and sealed with better blood (the blood of God Himself!). We, the New Covenant believers, have been given new hearts, not hearts of stone but hearts of flesh, with the law of the Lord written on it. The perfect love of God has cast out fear, and our confidence is in Him.

I contend that our New Covenant baptism, also called the baptism of the Holy Spirit, was not at the Red Sea but at the Jordan River. The Promised Land, a place of rest from works of the law, is to be enjoyed today (Hebrews 4:6-7), not in "the sweet by-and-by." If you live in new creation, you have crossed out of Old Covenant life and followed Yeshua into the Promised Land. The flooding river of inherited sinful nature that would have drowned you has been stopped up. The turbulent flow from Adam that once swept you away from your promised inheritance has been dammed. You now eat crops you did not plant, live on land you did not cultivate, and inhabit a city you did not build. This is grace. This is the New Covenant. This is the Gospel. This is new creation!

Now, at the risk of this being labeled a trouble-free, pie-in-the-sky understanding of the Good News, let me pause to point out that Jesus warned His followers they would face persecution, sorrow, rejection, and tribulation. That is the condition of the fallen world we have been commissioned to help restore, but in our Lord Jesus we find peace, and we can be of good cheer, because He has overcome the world. The Apostle Paul mentions suffering as a follower of Jesus more than a dozen times in his epistles, sometimes referring to his own suffering, sometimes referring to our suffering. Hope, however, is found in 2 Corinthians 1:5: "For as we share abundantly in Christ's sufferings, so through Christ we share abundantly in comfort too." What's more, Christ endured suffering in order to bring liberation to those enslaved in sin. If we share in that cup of suffering, may we endure to see others brought to salvation.

No, following Jesus is not trouble-free, but I promise you this, the troubles don't compare to the joy. The exhaustion of standing in faith only makes the victories that much sweeter. God is for you, not against you. He is not persecuting you. He is not causing your troubles, the world and its principalities are. In some cases, you're causing yourself trouble by not trusting Him, either by becoming entangled in sin or by putting confidence in your flesh. Remember, the Lord is giving you the grace you need to persevere in times of suffering. One of my favorite passages in scripture is Romans 5:1-5 (ESV). It says:

"Therefore, since we have been justified by faith, we have peace with God through our Lord Jesus Christ. Through him we have also obtained access by faith into this grace in which we stand, and we rejoice in hope of the glory of God. Not only that, but we rejoice in our sufferings, knowing that suffering produces endurance, and endurance produces character, and character produces hope, and hope does not put us to shame, because God's love has been poured into our hearts through the Holy Spirit who has been given to us."

We have peace with God, a peace won by Jesus, and not like the world gives. A worldly peace depends on an uneasy truce that is broken as soon as a shot is fired. God's peace depends on His righteousness, His faithfulness to us through the New Covenant, ratified by the shedding of Christ's blood. Now, with faith in our hearts, we have obtained access into the grace by which we stand. We have made it to the Promised Land. Fellowship with God has been restored, and we belong to a family again.

There are still giants in the land, but the old rules, tools, and weapons for dealing with them are ineffective. The old means of victory based on self-reliance and willpower are outmoded and obsolete. You now live by faith in God. You rely completely on His provision. Your strength comes solely from His indwelling Holy Spirit. You no longer subsist on a dull diet of manna, but feast on Jesus, the Bread of Life, the Living Word. He has prepared a banquet for you in the presence of your enemies. You follow His voice, His instruction, even when it sounds absurd (as it often will, when filtered through the wisdom of the world). You possess the land He has given you by defeating the enemy trying to share your inheritance, but you battle from a place of rest! It's a reflection of our heavenly reality of being seated with God in Christ (Ephesians 2:6). We still have work to do, the glorious partnership with the Lord in the labor of the Gospel, but again, we're not working to attain rest, we're working from a place of rest.

The Weapons of Our Warfare

"Okay, soldiers, gather 'round! Listen up. Our objective is a heavily fortified city. It's got a massive stone wall around it, and it's full of resistant citizens who absolutely do not want us to succeed in conquering them. Knowing that, the plan is to march around the city once a day for six days with the priests blowing trumpets, then march around seven times on the seventh day, then we'll blow some trumpets and shout. After that, the walls will fall down and we will be victorious. Any questions?"

How ridiculous did the strategy for conquering Jericho sound to the people of Israel? It's absurd even now to our ears, but those were indeed God's marching orders. Certainly it must have felt absurd to them in the midst of fulfilling God's instructions. One thing is sure, there were no doubters when the dust cleared and Jericho's walls had been reduced to rubble.

That victory, described in the sixth chapter of the book of Joshua, bolstered the faith of the Israelites and their confidence in God. However, there were more enemies to be conquered, including the giants that put fear and unbelief in the hearts of Israel forty years before. As they learned through defeat in the battle of Ai, immediately following the conquest of Jericho, there was no formula for victory outside of trusting God. We don't succeed by following a how-to manual. We walk by faith and not by sight. We listen to the Spirit's voice. His power is within us, His guidance on our hearts and minds. He's leading us to victory. We have only to follow.

But you must change your way of thinking. You must renew your mind and see things (including yourself) the way

God does. You must consider, reckon, and believe that God's declarations over you trump your own perceptions, opinions, theories, and circumstances. How do you defeat something bigger and stronger than you? Submit in faith to One bigger and stronger than any foe you will ever face. Trust Him. Obey Him, even when it sounds or feels absurd. Seek Him, inquire of Him, even when you think you know the way forward. You cannot beat an addiction through willpower. You beat it supernaturally. Your own virtue will not enable you to truly forgive someone who has nearly ruined your life. You forgive supernaturally. You cannot show love to someone who vehemently hates and opposes you. You love supernaturally.

Giants in the Land

Today, there are giants standing in the way of our inheritance of abundant life. These are enemies that stand in they way of us knowing the Lord's shalom peace in every area of our lives. They seem too huge and immovable for us to defeat. Maybe the giant you face is an addiction, a broken identity, an obstacle to a dream, a sickness, or a fractured relationship. Maybe the giant is poverty, a devastating circumstance, a tragic loss, or a traumatic memory. Do not repeat the doubting spies' mistake of unbelief as you try to size up your opponents. They believed they looked like grasshoppers in the eyes of the giants. The would-be conquerors were deterred by a lack of faith in God who *promised* them the land, and this unbelief afforded the giants another generation's worth of existence and expansion.

In your life, Jesus stands at the ready to help you drive out the giants and inherit the abundance He has for you, and the battlefield is your mind. He has already conquered the most brutal and tenacious enemies of sin and death for you. They cannot keep you from Him. He now offers you the armor of God (Ephesians 6:10-18). Put it on! Renew your mind and be transformed! The Lord wants you to rest. He wants you to enjoy the milk and honey and fruit of His provision. He has it waiting for you, and has assured and secured the victory, but you must trust Him and walk by faith, not by sight.

At the same time, the Enemy relentlessly employs his schemes to take your eyes off Jesus and His promises. He uses your situation or circumstances to convince you God isn't for you, or that you're not fit for battle (eyes on a lie, eyes on your shame). He redirects your focus and efforts by showing you what you need to fix, and offers a self-help manual that puts all your confidence in your flesh (eyes on your lack, eyes on a command). Turn your eyes from those distractions. Fix your eyes on Jesus.

It's not difficult to spot the differences between a performance-based, self-willed approach to life and a life of complete trust in the Lord. In the performance mindset, all we focus on is ourselves. We either see ourselves as too messed up to be any good to anyone else, and if despair doesn't take us down, we spend all our time on self-willed self-improvement, or we see ourselves as our own saviors and continue on a path of self-reliance and self-confidence. Remember the bride on her wedding night? She missed out on the fruitfulness of intimacy with the groom because she believed she was unpresentable and needed to fix herself. Jesus sets us free from both of these lies and calls us into intimacy with Him, but the call of the Gospel through Jesus extends beyond us. The Gospel involves our own salvation, of course, but it also commissions us to preach liberty to the captives. Claiming the land means pulling down strongholds of the enemy, yes, in your personal life initially, but as we step into the great commission, we pull down strongholds in the lives of others, too. Unlike Adam, we don't throw Eve under the bus when she eats the forbidden fruit, instead we appeal to her and show her the fruit of the Tree of Life, Jesus! Again, this ministry of reconciliation is done through the power of Christ within you, and the victories Jesus helps you win will be victories for others, too! This is what Paul speaks of in Ephesians 4:15-16:

"Rather, speaking the truth in love, we are to grow up in every way into Him who is the head, into Christ, from whom the whole body, joined and held together by every joint with which it is equipped, when each part is working properly, makes the body grow so that it builds itself up in love."

The Battle Belongs to the Lord

In the last segment of Exodus 23, God reveals His plan for Israel to occupy the Promised Land. These words were spoken well before the spies entered the land and the people were consumed with fear and unbelief from their report. These words resonate today. In verses 31-33, God says:

"...I will give the inhabitants of the land into your hand, and you shall drive them out before you. You shall make no covenant with them and their gods. They shall not dwell in your land, lest they make you sin against me; for if you serve their gods, it will surely be a snare to you."

In this life you've been invited into, this promised land place of rest, you have three choices: 1) Trust God to fight alongside you as you take on giants by faith, 2) settle for only a portion of your inheritance while the giants stay on your land, steal your provision and plot your ruin, or 3) wander in the wilderness outside of God's rest in fear and failure until your days are no more. The Holy Spirit will reveal to you the choices, patterns, habits, strongholds, and identities you're trying to live with that are not from Him and do not lead to abundant life. Do not make peace with those things. Do not try to coexist with them. Do not share your inheritance with them. Do not let them be a snare to you. Do not let them disturb your rest in the Lord. Drive them from your land with the weapons of the Spirit.

Listen to His voice. Trust His Word.

As Caleb said, you are well able to possess the land, and you can share his confidence because of your faith in the same God. You can share his success as the only one to rid his territory of all enemies, because the battle belongs to the Lord. The enemy knows the power of God within you and is afraid of you! Remember the report of Rahab while hiding the spies in Jericho? In Joshua 2, Rahab tells them the fear of God's people had fallen on the inhabitants of Canaan when they learned of God parting the waters of the Red Sea. The Canaanites heard how God had dried up Israel's opposition and routed their enemies during the journey, and the citizens of Jericho lived in dread that the Israelites were headed their way. What effect do you think that had on the spies' confidence?

In the same way, Satan knew his defeat was secured after the crucifixion and resurrection of Jesus. All that remains is the reclamation of the territory and eviction of the enemy. He knows his days are numbered and that he cannot vanquish the army of the Lord. He knows his gates will not prevail against us. He knows that his weapons won't prosper. Because of this, he resorts to his arsenal of deception, using lies, trickery, and propaganda to convince us that the promises of God aren't true or don't apply to us because we have violated the terms and conditions of the agreement with God. Praise God, the terms and conditions of our covenant with God are based completely on the faithfulness of Jesus and our faith in Him.

The Glory of the New Covenant

My friend Tom Green likes to illustrate the superiority of the New Covenant over the Old by talking about halogen headlights. When they first hit the scene in 1962, halogen lamps were a dramatic improvement in brightness and durability from the older car headlights being manufactured. You could light up a highway at night like never before. Of course, at high noon, you could have your high beams on and you wouldn't even be able to tell they were shining. Such is the comparison of the Old and New Covenants. The Old Covenant was bright, especially in the darkness of fallen creation. God's covenant people, Israel, were to be a light to the nations. But then came Jesus, and those who sat in darkness saw a great light. With the arrival of the New Covenant through Jesus, the true light of the world, darkness was dispelled, and the darkness will never overcome His light. Indeed, what once had glory has come to have no glory at all, as Paul discusses in 2 Corinthians 3.

Beginning to Believe

In my own life, receiving revelation of life in the New Covenant was revolutionary to how I walked, talked, and thought. The Good News was truly good, and I longed for clear and fresh ways to communicate its goodness with others. Being a fan of movies, I went on the lookout for New Covenant analogies while watching them. By far, the best analogy I have found is in the Wachowski brothers' film *The Matrix*. While I cannot recommend it for younger viewers, I really see the Gospel reflected in the themes of the film.

As the film begins, the main character Neo believes himself to be living a normal life, but soon discovers, with the help of people wanting him liberated from the Matrix, that his life has been a sham of sensual illusions propagated by a parasitic empire that draws its power from the enslavement of humanity. Sounds a bit like spiritual warfare, doesn't it? When Neo gets freed from the deceitful Matrix and receives training, he recognizes that to free others trapped inside, he must reenter its false reality and combat the powers that be. The big difference, and my favorite aspect of the Gospel analogy, is he is no longer governed by the rules of the Matrix and can therefore behave in supernatural ways. He can dodge bullets, jump over buildings, and wield some blindingly fast Kung Fu on the bad guys. The turning point in Neo's development and understanding of who he is comes as he no longer runs in fear from his nemesis, but instead faces him in battle. Neo's mentor Morpheus gloriously announces, "He's beginning to believe." From that point on, Neo no longer has to dodge bullets, he only has to hold up his hand and say "no" and the bullets stop in midair before dropping harmlessly to the ground.

And so it is with one born of the Spirit, living in the New Covenant. We no longer accept the limitations of the flesh. We can stop the fiery darts of the Enemy. We can do supernatural things like forgive those who have wronged us. We can pray for those who persecute us. We can bear with one another patiently. We can withstand the familiar temptations of the lust of the flesh. And we are more than conquerors! It takes some time to get strong. It takes some training. It involves the renewing of the mind and receiving revelation as you commune with the Holy Spirit. But once you feel the strength of the Lord working through you and see how it subverts the Enemy, you too will start to believe.

In the final scene of the movie, reminiscent of Jesus' great commission, Neo puts the enemy on notice that he's coming to rescue those caught in deception and darkness. We have not only been rescued, we have been sent out to rescue.

Liberty to the Captives

When the Allied Forces broke through Nazi defenses at The Battle of Normandy, it was the beginning of the end of World War II in Europe. As the Allies advanced through Europe, the Nazis, knowing they were beaten, rushed to exterminate as many concentration camp detainees as possible. It's an ugly but fitting analogy. Our enemy is defeated, but he's trying to make life a living hell for those imprisoned in sin. We, the forgiven and freed, are now part of a liberation force.

The Gospel provides a deep intimacy with God that goes way beyond personal fulfillment into a commission to preach liberty to the captives and open the doors of those in prison. Claiming the land means pulling down strongholds of the enemy, yes, in our own lives initially, but as the Spirit strengthens us as overcomers, we can show others how to pull down strongholds in their lives as well. This is the supernatural progression of grace. We receive it for ourselves, and as we rest, grow, and mature in the Lord, He shows us how to extend His grace to others. And on and on the family of God grows and His triumphant kingdom expands.

My Sheep Know My Voice

Perhaps the single most beautiful treasure restored to us through the work of Jesus is the ability to hear God's voice. Pastor Alan Hawkins teaches about Israel asking Moses to be their mediator, as the voice of the Lord was too terrifying for them. God honored their request and did not speak to His people except through prophets. That silence lasted until Jesus arrived. Now, the sheep can hear the voice of the Good Shepherd. Not just written text, not just canonized scripture, not just letters carved in stone, but the Living Word of God, Jesus, speaking to us through His Spirit. His law is written on our hearts and minds. His words of love, hope, joy, and peace are spoken in dreams, in visions, in nature, in words of encouragement and edification from a sister or brother, in songs, and in a still, small voice.

The long silence of God, starting at Mount Sinai, has ended, broken by the cries of Emmanuel, laying in a manger in Bethlehem. John, the voice of one crying in the wilderness, hailed Him as the Lamb of God who takes away the sins of the world. Jesus walked among us and showed us the face of

God. God audibly spoke His favor over His Son on multiple occasions. At the cross, He showed us the grace of God. At the resurrection, He showed us the power of God. Jesus became a curse to undo the curse, He became sin to defeat sin, and He rose from the dead to defeat death. Now, He shows us a new way of living, in a New Covenant and new creation.

Chapter 5
NONE THE WORSE FOR ADAM'S CURSE

Adam's fall killed us all, so the saying goes. Through his disobedience, humanity, all of creation in fact, was subjected to death. The curse of death can be felt not only in the brief number of our days, it can be felt in disease. It can be felt in famine. It can be felt in pestilence. In can be felt in the hatred, division, and selfishness of mankind. It can be heard in man's words of anger, wrath, malice, and slander. It can be heard in the frequently uttered words, "I'm only human." Borrowing again from Dr. Alan Hawkins, death is manifested in alienation, separation, expiration, and termination.

Adam was given love, companionship, and purpose. God gave him the tasks of naming the animals and tending the garden. God walked in fellowship with Adam and Eve in the cool of the day. With one act of disobedience, Adam squandered away a life of sole-dependence on God. The consequences were deadly.

In a recap of Romans 5, through one man, sin came into the world with death right behind. Through one man, judgment came, and following judgment was condemnation.

Jesus came with a solution. Although the Sermon on the Mount surely perplexed Jesus's listeners by adding to the difficulty of the law, more law was not the solution. Though

Jesus had multiple encounters with people whose sins He forgave, leaving them in their condition enslaved to sin was not the solution. To fulfill the law and then atone for mankind's sin was the solution. The solution was for God to resurrect a new creation race, commissioned to reconcile the fallen world by the power of the Spirit who raised Jesus from the dead.

Romans 5 contrasts Adam's disobedience with Jesus's obedience. Instead of a trespass that condemned everyone, Christ offers the free gift of righteousness and abundant grace to all who call upon the name of the Lord.

Where do we first see the newly risen Jesus, the last Adam? We first see him in the garden, being mistaken for a gardener. Was he tending the fruit? Stopping to smell the roses? I love the image of Jesus standing in the garden after crushing the head of the serpent, and picking up where His plan was interrupted with Adam and Eve.

What Adam lost, Jesus has restored in greater measure. Through Jesus, we tend the fruit of a spiritual garden, the always-in-season fruit of love, joy, peace, patience, kindness, goodness, gentleness, faithfulness, and self-control. Through Jesus, God allows us to use our creativity as we co-labor with Him, as Adam did naming the animals. Through Jesus, we walk again with God in fellowship, and our relationships with one another are life-giving as well. The curse of sin is broken. The curse of death is broken. Alienation, separation, expiration, and termination are nullified by reconciliation, communion, restoration, and resurrection. When we look back through scripture with New Covenant lenses, we learn this was God's plan all along.

The Gospel and the First Miracle of Jesus

In the account of the wedding at Cana in John 2, we see a profound foreshadowing of God's plan. Jesus, His mother

Mary, and His disciples had been invited to the wedding. The guests had gathered for the typical weeklong celebration of the wedding, but the mortified groom was in a quandary. Among his responsibilities were to keep the guests entertained and to make sure they had plenty to eat and drink, but he ran out of wine (that's what you get for inviting a bunch of fishermen to the wedding, my buddy R.K. Castillo says).

Following Mary's request for help, Jesus instructed the servants to fill the ceremonial washing pots with water, then He had a servant draw out water that had miraculously been changed to wine to take to the Master of the Feast. The Master, who did not know from where the wine came, tasted it and praised the groom for saving the best for last.

Now put yourself in the groom's place. You are full of anxiety that the guests who came to honor you have not been adequately accommodated. That is your fault. Despite your best efforts, you have failed. The Master of the Feast calls for you, and you approach, dreading his words of rebuke at your shortcoming. Instead of scorn, he praises you for not serving your best wine first, but for saving the best for last. Now you are really scratching your head because you provided your best and it ran out. Who is responsible for producing this new wine? Jesus. That is the Gospel, friends. The Old Covenant was not only incapable of covering our failures, it amplified them. But the New Covenant gets the real party started as Jesus produces superior fruit in and through us, while God gives us the credit!

How beautiful that Jesus sets the tone of His ministry in such a celebratory and gracious manner. John writes that this was the first sign through which Jesus revealed His glory. Oh, what a foretaste of glory divine!

Mercy and Grace

Let me illustrate this insight further. My wife and I have

a good friend from our college days named Jenny Hammit. One day I was lamenting to Jenny the devastating grade I had just received on an assignment for one of my classes. I knew there were not many grades taken for this particular course, and this paper would negatively affect my grade point average. I recall the professor's red-inked comment on my paper being something to the effect of "Well-written, but you did not follow the assignment." Hearkens back to Cain's sacrifice, does it not?

"On the bright side," I told Jenny, "the professor is letting me rewrite the paper, so at least there's some grace."

"No, that's mercy," Jenny said without missing a beat. "Grace is when the professor rewrites the paper for you."

I've heard mercy and grace contrasted in this way: mercy is not getting what you deserve, grace is getting what you don't deserve. The professor did not count my sin against me, but I was still responsible for correcting my condition. But Jesus, knowing we did not have the nature or strength to remedy our sinful condition supplied what we needed by His glorious grace. He aced the assignment for us. He knew exactly what was required, and He delivered. He took the test that we had failed miserably, and He passed with flying colors. He was faithful when we couldn't be, and what's more, He put our names at the top of the page. He gave His best, and He let us get the credit for it. Then He went further and deposited His Spirit into us, empowering us to live as overcomers. This is God's gift of grace by faith. As we received Christ by faith, Colossians 2 says, we continue to walk in Him by faith.

God Is in a Good Mood

My friend Tom Green thinks the parable of the prodigal son should be titled the parable of the rejoicing father. It's easy for us to make the prodigal the central figure in the story, since we relate to his waywardness and the misery of living in sin, but the remarkable part of this story is how the father responds to his son's return. Please hear me. God is in a good mood because you were lost and now you're found. Why is He rejoicing? Because you were stolen at birth and He found you and called out to you. When you answered, He adopted you and now wants you to undo your old ways of thinking. He wants you to renew your mind from the training of your old father, the Father of Lies. He wants to show you love, even though your old father said you were unlovable. Abba doesn't even want to hear your excuses; He wants to clothe you in your identity of being the King's child and heir.

Tom was the first person to tell me God was in a good mood, but the message has taken root in many hearts, and the number grows daily. At New Life City, where I serve as an associate pastor, we have a ministry team that journeys to New Orleans each year for Mardi Gras. Led by veteran street minister John Scholz (who has been showing God's love at the event for over thirty years), team members hold signs declaring the goodness, grace, and compassion of God. In direct contrast to the brutally condemning words on the signs of others who trumpet the anger and wrath of God, the signs held up by John and his team get the party-goers' attention. Curiosity piqued, many approach and ask what the signs mean, and a door is opened for the Gospel of grace to be shared. John and the team believe God's love speaks louder than megaphones. Written in colorful letters and joyous strokes, one sign declares "God Is In A Good Mood!"

Is that a bold statement? Here are some more: God is not uptight. God is not easily offended. God is not repulsed by our sin and fallenness like some divine germaphobe who finds us disgusting and detestable. God's heart breaks for the deceived who have paid with their lives to purchase counterfeit pleasures and a false identity from the Father of Lies. The Word became flesh and dwelt among us. The Word hung out with fishermen, prostitutes, and tax collectors. The Word broke bread and shared table fellowship with known sinners and other riff-raff. The Word did not properly wash before eating dinner with the Pharisees (and boy, did they notice). The Word walked through the wheat fields with his disciples "harvesting grain" on the Sabbath. The Word showed us divine love, and that love brought us to life. The Word was the light and life of man.

I know I risk coming off as irreverent or cavalier with this manner of talk, but all it takes is a smidgen of the leaven of the Pharisees to affect the whole ball of dough, and we must be on guard against it. It is time we start agreeing with our Abba. It is time we start declaring His truth over us. Not emotion. Not circumstance. Not other people's verdicts. God's truth. God's declarations. God's understanding. You shall know the truth, and the truth shall set you free!

And Such Were Some of You

"I am just a sinner, saved by grace."

This is what I'm talking about. How many times have you heard this phrase uttered? How many times have you uttered it yourself? It seems harmless, mildly self-deprecating, and even humble. But it misses the point of new creation. God identified Himself to Moses as "I Am." Jesus used "I Am" to identify himself in the Garden of Gethsemane. This is strong, declarative language. Scholars believe the use of "I Am" by the Lord was a statement of nearness, a word of comfort to the anxious and apprehensive Moses. Why would we use the language of "I am" to identify ourselves as something God has crucified and laid in the tomb with His son? You were a sinner, to be sure. You were. But by the grace of God after following Jesus in the likeness of His death and burial, we share not only Christ's resurrection, but His righteousness. Paul puts it like this in 1 Corinthians 6:9-11:

> "Do you not know that the unrighteous will not inherit the kingdom of God? Do not be deceived: neither the sexually immoral, nor idolaters, nor adulterers, nor men who practice homosexuality, nor thieves, nor the greedy, nor drunkards, nor revilers, nor swindlers, will inherit the kingdom of God. And such were some of you. But you were washed, you were sanctified, you were justified in the name of our Lord Jesus Christ and by the Spirit of our God."

Most of us are familiar with the concept of self-fulfilling prophecies. Studies show that the voice you most readily respond to and believe is not your mother's, your spouse's, your coach's, or your boss's. The voice you most often believe is *your own*. If you constantly tell yourself you're a bad parent or you're no good with money or you're never going to finish that project you started weeks or months or years ago, what happens? You start to believe it. When you start to believe something, you start to live it out. You start to behave as though what you're telling yourself is true. You may have plenty of reason or evidence to support your belief. You most likely have no reason to believe anything will change. You resign yourself to the declarations you've made over yourself and try to find a way to coexist with your failures. That's not abundant life, is it?

Change your confession. "I was a sinner, killed by grace, but now, thanks be to God, I *am* new creation!" Your use of the phrase "I am" is also a declaration of God's nearness and comfort in your life, of the transformation He has started and will complete!

The New You

For the majority of my childhood, you'll recall, I was the smallest boy in my class. Even after hitting my growth spurt and going from 4'11 and 73 pounds in 9th grade to 6'1 and

123 pounds in 12th grade (or from short and skinny to tall and skinny), I still thought of myself as the short kid. My personal perception shifted one day in the Air Force while getting ready to play a pickup basketball game at the park. As teams were being chosen, a guy I'd never met looked in my direction and said, "We'll take the tall guy." I looked around for the tall guy, only to discover he was talking about me! Tall guy, eh? No one had ever referred to me in that way before. Yeah, I liked the sound of that. And that was that. From that day on, I no longer thought of myself as the short kid.

Remember how God first looked at you when you returned from your prodigal wanderings. He saw you covered in filth. He smelled the stench of bad decisions on you. He had watched you walk away from Him. And what did He do when you came back? He embraced you! He kissed you! He arranged for you to be adorned in fine clothing, shoes, and the family jewelry! Then He threw a party to celebrate your return. YOU WERE WASHED! YOU WERE SANCTIFIED! YOU WERE JUSTIFIED! Jesus did this. The Gospel did this. You have a new identity!

If you've seen the film *The Princess Diaries*, you know the story of an awkward outcast of a girl who finds that she's actually the member of a royal family. She doesn't dress, talk, or act in a royal manner-- at first, anyway. But over time, and with constant reminders of who she is, she transforms into a beautiful, confident, composed young lady with legitimate authority. The same happens to us when we believe the report from our Father that we are now members of His royal family. We don't mope around with slumping shoulders and eyes to the floor. We hold our heads up. We revel with our Father. And guess what else happens when we're not sulking and looking at our failures? We are able to look around and see the plight of those who are not in the family. Then we engage in one of the greatest joys of the Kingdom: telling the orphaned spirits about Abba and introducing those lost souls to the King and His family.

The Curse of the First

I was the firstborn son in my family. Though my older sister Delena received all the fanfare for being the first girl born to the Elmore family in four generations, I still had the honors of being "Man of the House" when my dad was away (a title of which I reminded my little brother Clark quite regularly).

In the Old Testament, we see the tradition of honor, favor, and extra blessings bestowed on the firstborn son. But I also discovered an astonishing trend while studying sons, or more particularly, brothers. The trend is evident in the accounts of these well-known brothers from the Old Testament: Cain and Abel, Ishmael and Isaac, Esau and Jacob, Jacob's elder sons and Joseph, Ephraim and Manasseh, Aaron and Moses, Jesse's elder sons and David, and Absalom and Solomon.

With the exception of Ephraim and Manasseh (who are only mentioned briefly in scripture) and Absalom and Solomon, there existed obvious, interpersonal conflict between these brothers. That may be understating it with Cain, who murdered Abel. Ishmael mocked the newborn Isaac. Esau sought Jacob's life after Jacob swiped Esau's birthright and firstborn blessing. The sons of Jacob threw Joseph down a well before selling him to slave traders. Firstborn Aaron indulged in a brief spell of complaint and jealousy toward Moses. Jesse's sons despised and spoke harshly against David at the battle site shortly before he defeated Goliath. Absalom attempted to usurp his father David's throne, but it was Solomon who was King David's successor.

Beyond the conflict, however, lies the trend: the rejection or demotion of the older brother, and the acceptance or promotion of the younger brother. A review of the previously mentioned brothers proves the point. Cain's sacrifice was rejected; Abel's sacrifice was accepted. Ishmael was not the son of God's covenant promise, Isaac was. Esau gave up his birthright, and Jacob (through devious methods and abetted by his mother Rebekah) received the firstborn blessing from Isaac. The sons of Jacob came impoverished and seeking help from Joseph, who had become second in power only to Pharaoh in all of Egypt and the surrounding lands. Ephraim, the second-born son, was given the firstborn blessing instead of Manasseh at the insistence of Jacob. Moses was given the mantle of leadership over Aaron. David was anointed king instead of the rest of Jesse's sons. Absalom was killed by spear and sword while hanging from a tree, and his younger brother Solomon, whose wealth and wisdom would surpass all others, eventually occupied the throne.

So what do we make of this? A closer analysis of these stories provides an astounding confirmation of the nature of the Gospel. I believe that the behaviors and subsequent rejection of the firstborn and the acceptance, favor, and blessing of the younger mirrors the New Covenant dichotomy of walking according to the flesh and walking according to the Spirit. Simply put, we see our old nature manifested in the firstborn and our new creation selves in the younger sons. Let us examine a few of these brothers more closely.

Cain and Abel

Cain was a farmer. Abel was a shepherd. Their conflict came to a head after both brought an offering before the Lord. Abel brought fat portions from the firstborn of his flock, while Cain offered fruits of the soil. The Lord looked with favor at Abel's offering but had no favor for Cain's offering. Cain was angry and dejected. God told Cain he would be accepted if he did what was right, but warned him that if he did not do what was right, sin was waiting to pounce. Cain did not heed the warning, and killed Abel.

There has been much speculation over the reasons for Cain's sacrifice and God's rejection of it. Some say that Cain's pride prevented him from going to his younger brother the shepherd to appropriate a sacrificial lamb. Some say Cain indignantly thought his sacrifice was just as good as Abel's, though it is implied that he knew better. What clues does the Bible hold? God tells Moses in Leviticus that the blood of a sacrifice represents life, and we see that getting God to accept Cain's sacrifice of fruits and vegetables is literally like trying to get blood from a turnip.

There is another significant reason in play as well. In Genesis 3, following Adam and Eve's fall, God pronounced curses over the serpent and over the soil. "Cursed is the ground because of you," He told Adam. Not only did Cain offer a bloodless sacrifice, his offering came from cursed soil. God could not accept his offering.

In the same manner, any offering from our flesh, any attempts at our own righteousness, any of our best efforts to earn favor are not acceptable, as they all originate from corrupt flesh. As the oft quoted Isaiah 64:6 declares, "All our righteous acts are like filthy rags." To drive the point home, filthy rags in this verse are synonymous with used menstrual cloths, which is a biological way to say our best efforts are fruitless, unfertilized, and won't produce life. Our righteousness comes solely from Jesus and His finished work. We, like Abel, put our faith in the blood of the Lamb, and receive the commendation of Christ's righteousness as our covering. Without faith, it is impossible to please God.

Ishmael and Isaac

When God made covenant with Abraham (then called Abram), He declared his descendants would outnumber the sands of the seashore and the stars in the sky. Abraham waited and waited for offspring, with no results. When Sarah volunteered her servant Hagar to bear a child for Abraham, Ishmael was born. But God told Abraham Ishmael was not the child of the promise. In true supernatural fashion, Isaac was born to the 90-year old Sarah and the 100-year old Abraham.

On the day Isaac was weaned, Sarah caught the teenaged Ishmael mocking him. She moved swiftly to protect Isaac's inheritance: she told Abraham he must get rid of Hagar and Ishmael. Though Abraham was grieved and conflicted, God told him to honor Sarah's request.

In Galatians 4, Paul tells his readers that Hagar and Sarah represent the Old and New Covenants respectively. Paul continues the analogy with the offspring of each woman (or covenant):

"But just as at that time he who was born according to the flesh persecuted him who was born according to the Spirit, so also it is now." Galatians 4:29

So Hagar, representing the Old Covenant, produces offspring the old-fashioned way. You can learn about that method in a middle school Biology class. Sarah, as the New Covenant, needed a miracle to give birth to Isaac, as she was 90 and obviously well beyond childbearing age. Science has no explanation for Isaac's birth. He was born according to the power of the Spirit of God. Born out of death, you might even say.

The New Covenant parallel is obvious, as Paul discusses. He tells us that those born according to the Spirit (New Covenant, new creation life) are the children of God's promise. There is no more union with the law, which only produces offspring that tries to share our inheritance while mocking our supernatural birth. Hagar is the law, Ishmael is works of the law, and Paul says to throw both out.

Another point Paul makes in the above scripture is those born according to the flesh persecute those according to the Spirit. Of course, we can apply this scripture to the world's persecution of those who follow Jesus, but I believe it is also true of the tension we feel within ourselves as we walk out our faith. As Paul says in Romans 7:22-23,

"For I delight in the law of God, in my inner being, but I see in my members another law waging war against the law of my mind and making me captive to the law of sin that dwells in my members."

Our flesh wars against our spirit, not only as we deal with the lust of the flesh, the lust of the eyes, and the pride of life (1 John 2:16), but also as we attempt to step out in faith, to take Kingdom risks, and to trust in the Lord. Our logic opposes and even tries to shame our reliance on God. Often our flesh mocks our spirits when we turn to the Lord instead of taking matters into our own hands, as Abraham did in the conception of Ishmael. Yes, in our flesh we can make things happen, we can create, we can bring things into being, but only the fruit from our union with the Spirit brings about the blessings of life, abundant and eternal.

Esau and Jacob

Esau and Jacob, twin sons of Isaac and Rebekah, had conflict even in the womb. As the babies wrestled inside her, Rebekah inquired of the Lord, and He told her that the babies were two nations or peoples. He also said the older son would serve the younger. Jacob came out second, clutching the heel of the hairy Esau, as if prophetically signaling he would not be left behind. Genesis 25 describes Esau as a skillful hunter and a man of the field, while Jacob was a quiet man who dwelled indoors.

One day as Jacob cooked stew in his tent, Esau came in

from the field exhausted and famished and asking for some of Jacob's stew. Jacob saw the opportunity and offered the food in exchange for Esau's birthright, or the larger share of inheritance at the time of Isaac's passing. Esau did not see the point of a birthright if he was about to die of hunger, so he traded it away for bread and stew.

This pattern of poor choices continued for Esau. He took three wives for himself of Hittite and Ishmaelite descent. This grieved Isaac and Rebekah, whose union came from Abraham's wishes to keep his descendants from marrying those outside of God's covenant lest they be swayed from following the Lord.

At the end of Isaac's life he told Esau to go hunting and prepare the game he killed to serve Isaac a meal. The meal was to be followed by Isaac giving Esau the blessing of the firstborn. Esau left to carry out his father's request, but Rebekah overheard and hatched a plan to disguise Jacob as Esau and receive the firstborn blessing. She had Jacob kill some goats for her to cook, then told Jacob to put on Esau's clothing. Jacob protested that he was not hairy enough for the ruse to succeed, but the ingenious Rebekah put the goatskins on Jacob's arms to complete the disguise and fool Isaac into blessing Jacob. Jacob had to flee for his life upon Esau's return and subsequent discovery of Jacob's swindle, and Esau was anguished to learn Isaac had but one blessing to give.

Christ, who knew no sin, became sin in order that the wrath of God for the sins of the world would be atoned for in Jesus. We who have been baptized into Christ, according to Galatians 3:27, have clothed ourselves with Christ. Just as Jacob received Esau's firstborn blessing by being disguised as Esau, so we, clothed in Christ, now receive the blessings of the firstborn from the dead; forgiveness, justification, sanctification, righteousness, unbroken fellowship with God, the presence of the indwelling Holy Spirit, the mind of Christ, eternal life, abundant life, and the list just keeps going!

Part of the blessing spoken over Jacob was that his brother would be his servant. If we continue the analogy of the firstborn representing the flesh and the second-born representing new creation life, we see a beautiful picture of our flesh serving our Spirit, and not the other way around. In Galatians 5:16 Paul says when we walk according to the Spirit we do not gratify the desires of the flesh. You have a choice now. You no longer have to submit to the tyranny of sin in your life. You *were* a slave to sin, but now you are a slave to righteousness. This passage further illustrates my point:

"You, however, are not in the flesh but in the Spirit, if in fact the Spirit of God dwells in you. Anyone who does not have the Spirit of Christ does not belong to him. But if Christ is in you, although the body is dead because of sin, the Spirit is life because of righteousness. If the Spirit of Him who raised Jesus from the dead dwells in you, He who raised Christ Jesus from the dead will also give life to your mortal bodies through His Spirit who dwells in you." Romans 8:9-11

Remember God's prophecy to Rebekah of the two nations or peoples within her womb? In addition to this foreshadowing the literal nations of Israel and Edom, I believe this also applies to the people born of flesh and the people born of the Spirit (a royal priesthood, a holy nation). The inheritance of those born of the Spirit is the blessing of God's presence, and the right to be called children of God. Only the reborn can receive the blessing. But for those like Esau, who have spurned the blessings to come in favor of the immediate gratification of the flesh, there is no inheritance. There is but the emptiness of living for this life only, the fleeting and terminal pleasures of self-indulgence.

"'I have loved you,' says the Lord. But you say, 'How have you loved us?' 'Is not Esau Jacob's brother?' declares the Lord. 'Yet I have loved Jacob but Esau I have hated. I have laid waste his hill country and left his heritage to jackals of the desert.' If Edom says, 'We are shattered but we will rebuild the ruins,' the Lord of hosts says, 'They may build, but I will tear down, and they will be called 'the wicked country,' and 'the people with whom the Lord is angry forever.'" Malachi 1:2-4

If you are reading this book and have only experienced the first birth, you may be feeling that the deck is stacked against you. Let me lift the heaviness of this passage with the hope found in the words of Jesus.

Jesus once had a secret meeting with a religious leader, a Pharisee named Nicodemus. Some of Christ's most well known words came from this conversation. While John 3:16 is one of the most referenced scriptures in the Bible, my favorite verses in this passage follow it:

"For God did not send His Son into the world to condemn the world, but in order that the world might be saved through Him. Whoever believes in Him is not condemned, but whoever does not believe is condemned already, because he has not believed in the name of the only Son of God." John 3:17-18

Jesus did not come to condemn us. We were already condemned due to our sinful nature and the law that revealed our guilt. Jesus came to save us. There is hope of new life for everyone, but you must be born a second time.

Chapter 6
HOW TO DEAL WITH SIN

So far in the book we've studied the scheme of the enemy to take our eyes off the Lord. We've compared the condemnation of Moses with the salvation of Jesus. We've learned how to enter into the Promised Land of rest from works of the law by faith in Jesus, and we've seen how the pattern of acceptance and rejection amongst brothers in the Old Testament underscores the importance of living according to the Spirit instead of remaining in bondage to the flesh. But what light does the New Covenant cast on the problem of sin and the sinful nature that wars against our spirits? If Jesus conquered sin and death, why are they still so present in our everyday lives?

Among the mysteries of God are that His kingdom has come and is still coming. We have been born again into New Covenant, new creation life, yet there is still fallenness all around us, and even within us. Part of the ongoing work of the Gospel in God's kingdom is to reclaim creation from this fallenness, and it starts with our own lives. By walking in faith in the power of the Spirit, we put to death the misdeeds of our old nature.

The Truth on Sin

In my opinion and in my experience, the area of the Christian life most focused upon by Christians (and by the world pointing out our hypocrisy) is the problem of sin. I get it. Our desire to be pleasing and acceptable to the Holy God drives us to constant self-improvement (the spirit is willing, but the flesh is weak). There are countless books, sermons, blogs, and teachings on the subject. There are also many well meaning but unscriptural beliefs about the topic of sin that need to be exposed as fraudulent and exchanged for Gospel truth. These practices, as Paul says about religious traditions in Colossians 2:23, have the appearance of wisdom but are of no value in restraining the indulgence of the flesh. They do not release you from the shackles of sin, but rather throw you, shackles and all, into a prison cell of religious striving.

In the broad range of teachings on the subject, there are also a variety of definitions for sin throughout the church. The translation of the word means to "miss the mark." Some say sin is violating the Ten Commandments or any part of the Mosaic Law. Some say sin is doing what you know you're not supposed to do (sins of commission), and not doing what you are supposed to do (sins of omission). In the fourth century, a list of seven cardinal or deadly sins, somewhat subjectively extracted from the study of scripture, emerged in the church. On top of all that, Romans 14:23 says whatever does not proceed from faith is sin.

While our definitions vary, we can inescapably agree that sin comes with consequences. What goes around comes around. Our actions cause reactions. Whatever we reap, we sow. When we plant seeds of anger, hatred, immorality, greed, selfishness, or vengeance, to name a few, those seeds grow into an unwanted harvest in our lives. Sin robs us of peace and slowly drains the life from us. It hurts us and it hurts those around us. It is a ravenous, soul-sucking monster that mere humans are powerless to stop.

In the first chapter I alluded to the piety of my younger days. I was truly sheltered, by the grace of God and careful guidance of my parents, from a lot of temptation common to other boys and young men. When sexual temptation finally beset me, it came at me with a vengeance. I tried valiantly and failed frequently in my attempts to weather the storm as I fought against lust and dishonorable thoughts. My head hung with guilt, my heart sunk low with self-condemnation, and I even started to question my own salvation.

Thinking I knew how to deal with sin, I turned to 1 John 1:9. Confess, ask for forgiveness (though the verse does not say to ask for forgiveness), be cleansed from all unrighteousness, and repeat. This happened again and again, until my apologies sounded hollow and unbelievable. My pledges never to repeat the transgression were unconvincing. I sought advice from others in the church, but the medicine they prescribed came with side effects, to include guilt, shame, condemnation, desperation, and worse, indifference, apathy, and rebellion. Only Jesus offers the cure.

If you have spent any time in this miserable state, I sincerely want to help you. Before I tell you how to deal with sin, let me tell you how *not* to deal with it.

Myths, Half-truths, and Home Remedies

I recall perusing my parents' bookshelves as a young boy. I was particularly fascinated by *The Foxfire Book* (and subsequent volumes), which recorded the oral tradition and wisdom of mountain folks living in the Appalachians of Northern Georgia. The books contained amazing photos of giant rattlesnakes, instructions on how to build chimneys or make moonshine, and a host of lore related to getting cured of various maladies. One memorable cure was for the common wart: extract blood from the wart, smear the blood on a penny, and leave the penny on the ground (bloody side down) for someone else to find. Your wart would disappear when a hapless person picked up your coin, only to reappear on the person who snatched your penny! I'm almost certain this cure is ineffective, but I steer clear of pennies on the ground for good measure.

Remedies like that amuse us and quickly draw our skepticism, but it bewilders me in our quest to deal with the problems common to man how much lore we find in modern church traditions. These traditions have been established and passed down for generations, centuries, and even millennia. While these traditions in some cases were derived from scriptural interpretation, they are not explicitly communicated in the Bible, and yet people treat them with canonical reverence.

If you will indulge me, I have put together a short quiz on the subject of sin and forgiveness. There's no shame involved, and I will not be collecting your answers or posting your score, so please answer honestly according to what you believe on the subject. Please note that if you mark in your book and later lend the book to friends, they will know your answers, so you can be sure your friends will find you out.

SIN AND FORGIVENESS QUIZ

Read each statement and answer true or false:

1. Christians are sinners saved by grace.

2. The Bible instructs us to confess our sins before taking communion.

3. The Holy Spirit convicts Christians of sin.

4. When you sin, you don't lose your salvation, but fellowship with God is broken.

5. It is a sin not to believe you have been forgiven.

6. God cannot hear the prayers of those with unconfessed sin in their lives.

7. To repent is to confess sins, apologize, and ask for forgiveness.

8. The sins of unbelievers have not been atoned for.

9. When you accepted Christ, all of your sins up to that point were forgiven, but sins committed after your salvation still require God's forgiveness.

10. When Christ returns, he's going to judge the world of sin.

That wasn't too hard, was it? Now let us look at what the scriptures have to say in response to these questions.

1. *Christians are sinners saved by grace:* **FALSE.**

The key word in this question is the verb "are" which indicates a current condition or status. Christians are no longer identified as sinners, but as saints. Paul goes through a long list of transgressors in 1 Corinthians 6:9-10 and concludes in verse 11 by saying "and such were some of you, but you were washed, you were sanctified, you were justified in the name of our Lord Jesus Christ and by the Spirit of our God." Christians *were* sinners saved by grace, now they are new creation in a holy race. The old has passed away, and behold all things have become new. Please do not overlook the importance of understanding your identity in Christ. To paraphrase Proverbs, as a man thinks, so he is. An important step in renewing your mind is declaring over yourself what God says about you. Do not call unclean what God has called clean!

2. *The Bible instructs us to confess our sins before taking communion:* **FALSE.**

I was raised in a church tradition that practiced confession of sins before every communion. We were often instructed to ask the Lord to reveal any unconfessed sin we had in our lives so we could confess it and ask for His forgiveness. If we failed to do so, we risked eating and drinking damnation upon ourselves. This tradition has its origins in 1 Corinthians 11:27-29, but earlier in the text, starting in verse 17, we learn that Paul was chastising believers who were excluding others, practicing divisions, and being greedy and uncaring gluttons and drunkards at the observance of the Lord's supper. Paul's outcry was against such brash selfishness being shown during the remembrance of the most selfless act humanity has ever seen. He was telling them to examine themselves to make sure the charity and grace Christ had shown them was being shown through them as well. Sadly, the twisting of these words has resulted in more divisions, and as in the story of my friend who was prohibited from partaking in communion, the exclusion is very damaging to the witness of Christ.

3. *The Holy Spirit convicts Christians of sin:* **FALSE**.

Yes, you read that correctly. It's not a typo. That statement is false. I've heard Christians talking with regularity about the Holy Spirit convicting them of sin, and yet nowhere in the New Covenant will you read of the Holy Spirit convicting believers of sin. Read it for yourself in John 16:8-9. The passage says the Holy Spirit, when He comes, will convict the world of sin, and righteousness, and judgment. It says explicitly that the Holy Spirit convicts the world of sin because *they do not believe*. Right on the heels of that, in an offer of hope, we read that He convicts of righteousness. This is good news because it shows that the Spirit is not coming only to point out our fatal flaw, but to provide salvation through the covenant faithfulness of Jesus, also known as righteousness. He convicts the ruler of this world, the Devil, of judgment. Maybe you feel I am being nit-picky, but the word convict means to declare someone guilty. This passage in John summarizes the work of the Spirit to point out the unbeliever's unrighteousness, reveal His own righteousness in providing salvation, and then judge the Devil.

The Holy Spirit also reminds believers of His faithfulness to God's covenant (righteousness) being reckoned to our account, in opposition to the Accuser declaring us guilty. Does the Holy Spirit reveal to us things in our lives that hurt us, issues to trust Him with, and temptations and struggles from which to flee? Yes, He does. Does He point out when our words or actions cause others or us pain? Yes, He does. But do not mistake the condemning, shaming voice of the Accuser for the voice of the loving, affirming, life-changing Good Shepherd. The Accuser raises a fuss about the stench of your buried, sinful nature. The Holy Spirit points to your new creation life, reminds you that you are the fragrance of heaven, and empowers you to live victoriously over sin.

4. *When you sin, you don't lose your salvation, but fellowship with God is broken:* **FALSE**.

I am not sure how this myth originated, but it is propagated in statements like this: "God will never stop being your father, and you will never stop being His child, but when you sin, you lose fellowship with Him." These phrases are uttered as though there was a giant revolving door into the Holy of Holies. One minute you are in the dwelling place of God, and the next time you sin, you are out.

I remember playing in the hot, Texas summertime of my youth, and I recall a commonly uttered phrase from my mother as my brother and I constantly retrieved a different toy from our room before returning to the outdoors.

"In or out. Choose one." Opening the front door let the flies in and the cool air out. During my struggle with recurring sin in my later life, that's the message I heard about God as well. You're either in His presence or you're out. But then I read this:

"For by the death He died, He died to sin [ending His relation to it] once for all; and the life that He lives, He is living to God [in unbroken fellowship with Him]. Even so consider yourselves also dead to sin and your relation to it broken, but alive to God [living in unbroken fellowship with Him] in Christ Jesus." Romans 6:10-11 (AMP)

Consider yourself dead to sin and alive to God. Reckon it to be so. If you cannot fathom it, then renew your mind and be transformed. As my friend Clifton Coulter says, "God does not know us the way we know ourselves." He does not see us like we see ourselves. God calls you alive to Him and dead to sin. Believe Him! Renew your mind! There is no revolving door in and out of the presence of God. There is only a torn veil, a description Hebrews 10:20 uses for Christ's body, through which we have entered the presence of God. We approach our Father through faith in Jesus and His death, burial, and resurrection.

When you sin, some contend, you don't lose your salvation, but you lose fellowship with God. This is an Old Covenant way of thinking. Isaiah 59:2, in a prophecy to Israel, says, "your iniquities have made a separation between you and your God, and your sins have hidden His face from you so that He does not hear." The chapter then foretells of a Redeemer coming to Zion.

The Redeemer has come. The Old Covenant has been made obsolete. The New Covenant has been ratified with the shedding of Jesus' blood. Could that be any plainer? Those in Christ must consider themselves dead to sin, and consider themselves living in unbroken fellowship with Him. Consider it. Reckon it. Put your faith in it. Be transformed by it.

I once heard a preacher tell a story to illustrate his belief that sin separates us from God. He used an analogy of a little boy who steals his father's pocket watch. His father knows good and well the little boy stole it, but he's waiting for the boy to confess. As long as the boy does not confess, he experiences broken fellowship and separation from his father. The father does not cease to be a father, the son does not cease to be a son, but this transgression prevents a peaceful relationship. As soon as the boy confesses, fellowship will be restored.

I understand the logic of the analogy, but a key figure is missing. Jesus is absent from this story. If you want to use the characters in this analogy, you must include an older brother who not only died to pay for every transgression the younger son ever committed or would ever commit, but who also lives again to show His little brother abundant life, and a Father who says, "Everything I have is yours!"

The Good News is so much better than we've let ourselves believe. For God not only sent Jesus to atone for us through His death while we were still sinners and enemies with Him, God's Spirit also raised Him from the dead! I could certainly understand feeling guilty and shameful in the sight of God if Jesus merely died for our sins. I would understand God holding a grudge toward us if Christ had not been raised. But He has been raised, and we with Him. Not as rehabilitated sinners but as new creation saints; holy, righteous, justified, sanctified, and equipped to be ambassadors of reconciliation to the world.

So what keeps us from enjoying this unbroken fellowship? What makes us feel God's presence in one moment and the absence of it the next? What fills us with grief, guilt, and shame? Why did we sin to begin with? Why can't we find relief for this madness? All of these questions have the same answer. Unbelief. This was the same thing that kept the faithless Israelites from entering their rest.

5. *It is a sin not to believe you have been forgiven:* **TRUE**.

If we are to take the Bible at its word, there are dozens of verses that speak of us having been forgiven (I've included 17 of them in the next chapter). The Bible also says in Romans 14:23 that whatever does not proceed from faith is sin. How it must break the heart of Jesus to have given His life for our forgiveness and freedom, and for us of little faith to not believe it's true and remain in the clutches of the Enemy's lies. Incidentally, you're even forgiven for not believing you're forgiven, so believe and enter rest from sin and striving!

6. *God cannot hear prayers of those with unconfessed sin in their lives:* **FALSE**.

This is not a trick question, and I am not trying to play with words here, but to those who insist on confession of sin as a condition for forgiveness, I ask this: how can God hear your prayer if He cannot hear the prayers of those with unconfessed sin? There are several verses in the Old Testament (namely Psalm 66:18 and Isaiah 59:2) that speak of God not hearing the prayer of the wicked, but the only place we see this verse mentioned in the New Testament is in John 9:31. In that verse, a man healed by Jesus of blindness is giving his testimony to the Pharisees. Obviously the cross changes everything, and the Lord is quick to hear anyone who calls out to Him.

7. *To repent is to confess sins, apologize, and ask for forgiveness:* **FALSE.**

Mark 1:4 in the Amplified Bible says this: "John the Baptist appeared in the wilderness (desert), preaching a baptism [obligating] repentance (a change of one's mind for the better, heartily amending one's ways, with abhorrence of his past sins) in order to obtain forgiveness of *and* release from sins." We see the definition of repentance is simply about changing your mind, turning around, and recognizing the destruction sin brought. Somehow through time and tradition, repentance has come to be synonymous with confession, remorse, apologies, and asking for forgiveness. Parents know as well as anyone that a child who says sorry 20 times a day for repeatedly disobeying has not had a change of heart. How many times have we said, "I don't want you to be sorry, I want you to stop disobeying!" You can be sorry, admit your faults, and ask for forgiveness and yet remain on the path of destruction. When you repent, you change your mind (renewing it to God's reality) and change your direction.

8. *The sins of unbelievers have not been atoned for:* **FALSE.**

If the sins of all mankind were not atoned for at the cross, what's the plan of atonement for those who have not yet received God's gift of salvation? Recall that Romans 6:10 says the death Jesus died to sin He died only once. John the Baptist called Jesus "the Lamb of God who takes away the sins of the world." In 1 John 2:2 we read that Jesus is "the propitiation for our sins, and not for ours only but also for the sins of the whole world." 1 Timothy 4:10 says, "For to this end we toil and strive, because we have our hope set on the living God, who is the Savior of *all people*, especially of those who believe." The sins of unbelievers have indeed been atoned for, but until they receive God's gift of salvation, they remain dead and entombed in the old nature.

9. *When you accepted Christ, all of your sins up to that point were forgiven, but sins committed after your salvation still require God's forgiveness:* **FALSE**.

Hebrews 9:22, echoing Leviticus 17:11, reiterates this divine principle: without the shedding of blood there is no remission of sins. Plain and simple, the sins of the world were remitted at the shedding of Christ's blood at Calvary 2,000 years ago. The atoning sacrifice was made once for all. Forgiveness is a done deal. All your sins were future sins when Jesus shed His blood on the cross. You received His gracious gift of forgiveness at the moment of your salvation and rebirth.

10. *When Christ returns, he's going to judge the world of sin:* **FALSE**.

One of my favorite bumper stickers reads: JESUS IS COMING, LOOK BUSY! It amuses me because for so long I lived in tension and fear, making sure I was doing right as much of the time as possible lest Jesus return in the midst of me breaking the rules. I definitely did not want to get caught hanging out in a bar, sneaking out after curfew, or watching an R-rated movie when Gabriel blew his trumpet. But read these amazing words in the Amplified Bible:

"Even so it is that Christ, having been offered to take upon

Himself and bear as a burden the sins of many once and once for all, will appear a second time, not to carry any burden of sin nor to deal with sin, but to bring to full salvation those who are [eagerly, constantly, and patiently] waiting for and expecting Him." Hebrews 9:28

Jesus is not coming back to deal with sin. Jesus did it right the first time. Remember Romans 6:10? He dealt with sin and forever ended His relation to it. When He returns, it will be to end our struggle with the flesh, to establish His kingdom in its fullness in, through, and to us, and to let us know Him as He knows us. Look eagerly!

I pray that quiz was an eye-opening and even life-changing experience for you. I know in my own life, believing mistruths and using ineffective, religious approaches to deal with sin kept me in a state of sin-consciousness and a mindfulness of my helpless estate. I simply could not believe any teaching of my true identity in Christ since that identity didn't align with my own negative self-confessions, and like the bride on her honeymoon, I believed the lies of the Enemy that Jesus didn't really want to be close to me. Sure, Jesus loved me, but there was no way He liked me. Once I believed Jesus removed every barrier that stood between us, I started to receive His pure love and grace for me, and transformation began. Of course, it took a while to renew my mind to His truths, but as I did, I started to recognize sin for the insidious and ravaging beast that it is.

Don't Kick that Dog

I was a wee Texan living in the city of Midland. One day, around age five, I went to my buddy Anthony's house for a play date. Anthony's mom took us over to her friend's house, with whom she visited while we played in the front yard. To the side of the yard was the family dog, a large, white, German shepherd mix. The dog was chained up and napping, head resting on

109

his front paws. I asked Anthony if the dog bit people. Anthony assured me that indeed it did, and told me we should leave it alone and get on with playing. With my curiosity satisfied for the moment, we continued to play, but before long I again asked Anthony about the dog.

"Yes, it bites!" He responded. "Now let's play!" Still unsatisfied with his answer, I half-heartedly continued to play.

I can't really explain what went through my mind shortly after that. I believe I was feeling indignant towards the dog about its tendency to bite people. I felt that since it was on a chain, I could teach the dog a lesson with little to no danger to myself. I confidently strode up to the resting dog in my wee Texan cowboy boots, sized up the dog (who was now sizing me up, too), took aim, and with all my might, kicked the dog in the head with the heel of my boot. It turns out I had miscalculated the reach of the dog's chain.

I think it's best to skip the gory details, but I will say the dog repaid evil for evil, and I was soon on my way to the ER to receive around seventy stitches in my scalp and right eyelid. In case you're wondering, I recovered quickly, I do not wear an eyepatch, and I love dogs and have not kicked one since.

For years I listened to my mom tell others that story, though her secondhand summation varied significantly. I had actually never given her my account, but she pieced details together like a crime scene investigator until she could make sense of it. Her version had me playing in the yard, going down the slide of the swing set, and colliding with the vicious dog awaiting me at the bottom of the slide. The dog had no recourse but to maul me. I never corrected her story as a child, since her deductive reasoning hid my moronic actions and put me in the role of innocent victim. It was only in my later teen years that I told her what really happened. She preferred her version.

I've mused over that incident frequently through the years, until I made a connection between that story and the redeeming grace of Jesus. Before Jesus, sin ran around unchained, harassing and attacking at will, like a wild dog. It was up to us to overpower it. But through the finished work of Jesus, that sin nature has been put on a chain. You now have the ability, by the power of the Spirit of Jesus, to steer clear of that vicious beast waiting to tear you apart. What happens when you enter the radius of sin's chain? You are subject to attack. What happens when you toy with it (or even kick it)? It pounces on you. Remember God's words to Cain in Genesis 4:7? "If you do not do what is right, sin is crouching at your door, it desires you, and you must subdue it." God spoke these words to Cain before he took his brother's life. Obviously he couldn't subdue sin. And neither can we, apart from trusting the indwelling Holy Spirit.

The Burglar, the Dog, and the Slab of Meat

According to the logic of movies, the best way for a burglar to keep a ferocious guard dog from tearing him apart is to throw a slab of meat to the dog. While the dog munches happily away, the burglar can steal and plunder at will. Temptation is like the slab of meat (in this dog analogy, we are the dog). The thief comes to steal, kill, and destroy, but Jesus came to give us abundant life. What part of your abundant life is being robbed from you when you fall for the distractions of temptation? What is temptation trying to take your attention from?

Soon after this personal revelation, I found it very useful in dealing with temptation. My wife was teaching at a women's conference at our church, and I was home with our daughters. After putting them to bed, and finding nothing to do, I found myself open to the risk of temptation. Paul wisely warns us in

Romans 13:14 not to look for opportunities to feed the flesh. As I contemplated temptations, I remembered the burglar analogy. "What could the thief want to distract me from right now?" I asked myself. My thoughts instantly went to my wife teaching at the conference (though there are a host of things that giving in to even one temptation can steal from us). I turned from the temptation and prayed to the Lord for favor and blessing over my wife's ministry opportunity. She came home that night with testimonies of the mighty work of the Spirit as she ministered.

A Proper Response

So here we are, forgiven new creations, yet the sin nature still lurks in our body, according to Paul in Romans 7. How do we get victory? Old Covenant Israel experienced temporary relief on the Day of Atonement, but they longed for something more. They longed to be free from sin. The Day of Atonement dealt with sins for a year, but only served to remind Israel of their sins, much like April 15th serves to remind Americans that they owe taxes. Can you imagine the relief and jubilation the Day of Atonement brought, even if for only a day? What if we could enjoy right now an eternal condition of atonement?

Let me finally get to the point on the issue of how to deal with sin, as it is simply profound and profoundly simple: Jesus dealt with sin. We now deal with sin by believing that Jesus dealt with it! Praise Him! Thank Him! Trust Him! Call on Him! He has brought us into a new era where the jubilation doesn't end.

You are free to feel remorse when you blow it. You are free to apologize, but watch what happens when you, with a heart full of gratitude, thank Jesus for the complete gift of forgiveness. Watch what happens when you start to see sin, not as a good thing God is withholding from you, but as a prison cell on death row from which Jesus freed you. Watch what happens as you renew your mind to who you are in Christ, not a wretched sinner, but a saint, an ambassador of the Kingdom of God, an able minister of the New Covenant. Watch what happens when you move beyond what Hebrews calls the elementary doctrine of Christ, including repentance from dead works, and go on to maturity. Watch your prayers change…

"Thank you, Jesus, for setting me free from the bondage of sin. Thank you for giving me the satisfaction and fulfillment that sin promises but never delivers! Thank you for your gift of forgiveness. Thank you that I'm new creation, living in a New Covenant, living in unbroken fellowship with you! Thank you for showing me the path of life and for walking it with me. Thank you for the cross, and thank you for the empty tomb!"

Chapter 7
SINNER KILLED BY GRACE

When presented with the Gospel of grace, it is common to get overwhelmed with the richness of it and to think, "This is too good to be true." In our consumer-driven society, we are used to hearing grand promises accompanied by a list of restrictions in fine print. But it is not so with the Good News. *There is no fine print.* As Pastor Alan says, "Jesus gave His life for us so He could give His life to us so He could live His life through us." He came that we would have life to the fullest. Jesus removed all obstacles keeping us separated from His Father, and then His Father became our Father, adopting those who put their trust in Jesus! In Christ we are forgiven, we are justified, we are set apart for holy use (sanctified), and we are declared righteous. What's left is to continue in faith, and looking at Jesus, yield yourself to the transforming work of His Spirit who will conform you to His image from one degree of glory to the next!

Hold on, now. Let's not get carried away here. The type of message I'm preaching, if it falls into the wrong hands, will give people a license to sin, won't it? This message is okay for responsible people, but some folks will hear it and act foolishly, waving their "already forgiven" wand while not fearing reprisal. I hear your concern, and I completely understand it. But may I humbly suggest that the old way of trying to deal with your own sin also leads to a dead end? The old way depends on a constant sin consciousness. The old way tries to combat sin by adhering to the very law that will provide sin an opportunity to seize you and put you to death through that law. It's like trying to extinguish a fire with gasoline.

My friend Tom Green says people don't need a license to sin. They sin plenty without a license. Again, I can distill the essence of my message into this statement:

There is no life in sin. There is no life under the law. There is only life in the Spirit.

Remember, those who sin apart from the law die apart from the law. Those who sin under the law die under the law (and the law reveals us all to be sinners). We only find life, abundant and eternal, in the Spirit of God that raised Jesus from the dead. The law of the Spirit has set us free from the law of sin and death.

The people of God as defined by the New Covenant are not lawless. They walk according to the Spirit. They follow the law of the Spirit. They produce the fruit of the Spirit. There is life in the Spirit, but the letter of the law kills. I love how the Apostle Paul discusses this in 1 Corinthians 6:12 when he writes, "'All things are lawful for me,' but not all things are helpful. 'All things are lawful for me,' but I will not be dominated by anything." The people of God have one King, as Pastor Alan points out, and His name is Jesus. Freedom in King Jesus is freedom from the bondage of sin that brought us death. Freedom granted to us so we, as Zechariah prophesied in Luke 2:74-75, "…might serve Him without fear, in holiness and righteousness before Him all our days." This freedom, when accepted through faith, changes the way we see the schemes of the tempter.

One Little Monkey Jumping on the Bed

When young, we're told not to jump on the bed. It's fun but dangerous, and the rule, as we've learned, only intensifies the temptation. As adults, we don't jump on the bed because we see the risks to us AND the bed (and possibly the ceiling fan). We've also discovered the trampoline, something designed for this very pleasure, and can easily see the bed as a shoddy substitute.

For every tantalizing temptation that leads to one form of death or another, there is a superior delight to be found in Jesus. The mystery, the task, the quest is to search it out and find it. The first step is to refuse buying into the counterfeit. The second step is to plumb the depths of the mind of Christ, which is yours by virtue of faith, and find life, abundant and eternal.

Account Transfer Complete

As we encounter the perfect lovingkindness of Jesus, gratitude prompts us to make offerings to Him. Sadly, we are too often told that Jesus paid our debt and now we have to pay Him back, but the "good news" is that He's much kinder than our previous creditor and he offers a much more reasonable interest rate. This is wrong, friends. Jesus is NOT in the business of buying debts. He's in the business of settling accounts and canceling debts. He's in the business of restoration and investment. He not only paid off your debt completely, He added your name to His bank account and gave you full access! The grace message that has been declared in recent years, praise God, has shown us that we cannot earn favor with God or do anything to make God love us any more than He already does. And yet we don't fully believe that our debt has been paid and we go back repeatedly asking for what's already ours. The longer we go thinking we still owe Jesus, the longer we go missing out on the vastness of heaven's resources.

Further complicating the simplicity of the Gospel is the far-fetched notion of partial atonement. When you purchase something using the lay-away system, you initially pay a portion of the price owed (usually around twenty percent of the total value), after which you make regular payments at a set interval until the debt is settled. You do not receive or possess the item until the last penny has been paid. Such is the concept of atonement in many people's minds. As they see it, at the moment of your salvation, you received forgiveness for all previously committed sins. That's the down payment. After salvation, they say, you still need to receive forgiveness for the sins you commit on a regular basis. This view goes on to say your sins will never be completely atoned for because you will, of course, continue to sin, and that you'll only be free from sin once you die and leave your mortal flesh behind.

Is this how you see it? Is that what Jesus is doing up in heaven now? Is He constantly atoning for our sins? God told Moses in Leviticus 17:11 that without the shedding of blood, there is NO remission of sins. Is Jesus perpetually shedding His blood? What is the science behind that? If blood isn't shed, there is no forgiveness, so if we're asking again to be forgiven, where is the shed blood? What sort of spiritual transaction do we suppose happens when we are "appropriating" our forgiveness? If you cannot answer these questions, I challenge you to reexamine what you believe. Hebrews says the priestly duties of Jesus are accomplished! He offered His blood sacrifice once and for all and then sat down at the right hand of God! He's not doing sacrificial shift work, like the Levitical priests of the Old Covenant. His blood was shed. Our sins were remitted. He atoned for ALL SINS for ALL TIME, and then He said, "It is finished."

SINNER KILLED BY GRACE

Why Do We Ask for What's Already Ours?

Husbands, how many times have you proposed to your wives? For most of us, once was enough. Some had to persist a little more, but once we were married, did we continue to ask our wives to marry us? Silly analogy, perhaps, but imagine a man who cannot believe he is actually married and constantly asks his wife to marry him. Being that she's his wife, she has legally bound herself to him until death separates them. How can they get on to any meaningful connection in their relationship if the man does not believe the woman is his wife? And how exasperated is the wife at her thickheaded husband? In the same way, why do you constantly ask God, who forgave you in Christ at the cross, to forgive you? Believe you're forgiven and exchange sin-consciousness for Christ-consciousness.

We are the Bride of Christ. We are in union with Him! As long as we keep ourselves locked in the bathroom trying to get presentable while looking in the mirror of the Law (instead of looking in His loving eyes), we will not spend time in fruitful union with the Bridegroom.

Forgiveness and the Lord's Prayer

So how are we to read the Lord's Prayer? After the disciples asked Jesus to teach them to pray, He taught them this beloved and oft-recited prayer, found in Matthew 6:9-13:

"Our Father in heaven, hallowed be Your name. Your kingdom come, Your will be done, on earth as it is in heaven. Give us this day our daily bread, and forgive us our debts as we also have forgiven our debtors. And lead us not into temptation, but deliver us from evil."

In this passage, Jesus goes on to tell His listeners that if they forgive others' trespasses, the Father would forgive theirs, but the Father would not forgive them if they did not forgive others (Jesus also expresses the same sentiment in Matthew 18:23-35 and Mark 11:25-26). Doesn't this contradict the Good News of the grace of God?

To answer this question, I'll first roll out a fancy word: hermeneutic. This word simply means to interpret or explain. Everyone who reads the Bible has a hermeneutic, or a method of interpretation for reading the text, whether they realize it or not. The hermeneutic I use when reading scriptures prompts two questions for any given passage I'm studying: 1) Who is the original and intended audience? 2) How does it fit into the overarching New Covenant narrative? Following this method of interpretation helps me understand, for example, that the Mosaic Law is not a governing code for Christians, but rather it governed the Old Covenant Israelites and showed them the proper way to establish a nation, to protect the people in matters of health, justice, and interpersonal relationships, and to set up a temporary system of atonement until the Messiah came and created a new race of those born of His Spirit, living under His New Covenant.

Who was the original and intended audience of the Lord's Prayer? The disciples and covenant-keeping Jews listening to the teachings of Jesus were the original audience. Are modern-day Christians part of the intended audience to follow the directives of this prayer? I have to say both yes and no.

In this passage (as in the other passages in parentheses above) Jesus was speaking to those under the law. Can you imagine the Jews hearing Jesus tell them they had to forgive the Romans? Can you imagine them hearing Jesus tell them they had to forgive tax collectors (those villainous traitors who were getting rich off their countrymen as contractors of the Roman Empire)? In passages like these (many of which are found in the Sermon on the Mount), Jesus laid impossible tasks on His audience of covenant-keeping Jews, revealing their need for a savior. The New Covenant had not yet been ratified, nor had their sins been atoned for in finality at the cross. This answers the second hermeneutical question of how it fits into the overarching New Covenant narrative. Since this prayer preceded Christ's victory through the cross and the resurrection, it can be viewed as a legitimate petition to the Lord leading up to the cross. The disciples asked Jesus for instruction, and He knew the enormity of the task He was called to in order to accomplish the will of His Father. His prayer reflected this. Let's look at which parts of the Lord's Prayer have been answered.

Has God's kingdom come on earth as it is in heaven? No, not completely, though it's in process, and we've tasted the firstfruits of God's kingdom coming. Has God given us daily bread? Yes, He has given us Jesus, the Bread of Life. Has God forgiven us? Yes, He has. The Apostle Paul puts a Gospel twist on Jesus' words in Colossians 3:13 when he says, "Forgive as the Lord forgave you." Does the Lord lead us into temptation? No! Has the Lord delivered us from evil? Yes! We have been rescued from the kingdom of darkness and transferred into the kingdom of God's beloved Son (Colossians 1:13).

The Lord's Prayer and other passages that appear to contradict the Good News were spoken by Jesus to reveal to His original audience their need for salvation, for a New Covenant, and for a source of strength greater than human willpower, the power of the indwelling Spirit of God. Only by the Spirit of God can we forgive others as we have been forgiven.

The Misery of Not Believing Your Forgiveness

In Genesis 45, we read of Joseph, son of Jacob, revealing himself to his brothers in Egypt after a long period of separation from them. These elder brothers, you'll recall, hated Joseph because of their father Jacob's love for him and because his

121

dreams foretold their subservience to him. They plotted to kill him, threw him in a well, then reconsidered and sold him into slavery. Needing to cover their crime, they tore and smeared with animal blood the cloak their father had made for him and lied to their father that Joseph had been killed by wild animals. Now as second in command to Pharaoh, with his brothers vulnerably trying to buy grain to stave off the famine, Joseph finally told them who he was. Having every right to be wrathful and vindictive, Joseph responded to them in the opposite spirit and foreshadowed the glorious Gospel of Jesus. He kissed them. He implored them not to be grieved or angry with themselves. He absolved them of their sin against him. He reassured them that he would take care of them, their families, and their livestock. He treated them with undeserved kindness. He gave them grain but did not take their money. He spoke to Pharaoh on their behalf, and Pharaoh contributed to the blessing, telling them to go retrieve their father, wives, and children, even giving them wagons to do so. He furthermore clothed them in new garments and sent riches and gifts with them, instructing them not to worry about bringing their old possessions, since all their old things would be replaced by the newest and finest in Egypt. Pharaoh told Joseph to have his father and brothers settle on the best of the land. Upon their return, Joseph provided his father, his brothers, and their families with an abundance of food, even in the midst of a great famine. There was no sign whatsoever that Joseph harbored bitterness towards his brothers. Is this not a beautiful picture of the Good News?

But if we skip ahead to Genesis 50 (interestingly the first place in scripture the word "forgive" appears), we read that after the death of Jacob, the brothers discussed the possibility that Joseph's vengeance was abated only while their father lived. They sent a messenger to Joseph saying Jacob urged him to forgive his brothers' transgressions and sins. Joseph heard the message and wept.

This passage raises several questions. Why did Joseph weep? Was the message really from Jacob, or had the notoriously scheming brothers made up another story to save their skins? Why, after seventeen years of living in the grace and providence of Joseph, did his brothers still fear retribution? It is my opinion that Joseph's brothers fabricated this story, as Jacob knew Joseph enough to know that he kept no record of wrongdoing. If this message was truly from Jacob, wouldn't he have told Joseph himself when giving his deathbed blessing? I believe the brothers said this because they still feared Joseph's wrath. They could not fathom such a lack of vengeance or so thorough a forgiveness and would not have responded in kind had the roles been reversed. I believe Joseph wept because his brothers had not received his forgiveness and did not know his heart of mercy. I believe he wept because the fear his brothers lived in had enslaved them just as much as their evil deeds had once led to his own slavery.

This is our story, saints, and all too often we act as Joseph's brothers did. Do you think we would be living in the goodness and abundance of God had Jesus not forgiven us completely? Do you think we would have been called out of the land of famine and clothed in garments of Christ's righteousness if God still held a grudge against us? Does it grieve His heart to have us live in the fear that He is holding our trespasses and sins against us? Does it grieve His heart to hear us ask for the forgiveness He has already granted? Does it grieve His heart to see us in bondage to guilt, shame, and fear after He gave His beloved son Jesus to secure our freedom from such bondage? Fear has to do with punishment, but perfect love casts out all fear! The one who fears has not been made perfect in love, but the one who trusts bears the fruit of God's goodness.

Bubba's Berry Bush

We called my maternal grandmother Bubba. We loved to visit Bubba's house. Not only was she a delightful woman, she kept a treasure trove of junk food in her pantry (the foil-wrapped Hostess Ding-Dongs were my favorite). I remember a bush in her front yard full of shiny, orange berries. Bubba warned us not to eat those berries because they were poisonous and would make us very ill. We listened, but my young mind wondered why someone did not pluck all the berries off the bush and eliminate this poisonous threat.

I find that many Christians have the same approach in dealing with sin. Jesus said a tree is known by its fruit, and that a bad tree is not capable of producing good fruit. With an Old Covenant mindset, when we see poisonous fruit growing on our tree, we point it out to Jesus, ask Him to pluck it off, and continue as usual until we discover more of the same. The problem is much deeper than we think. The problem, of course, goes down to the roots. A poisonous fruit-bearing plant is ONLY capable of producing that type of fruit. The way to deal with such a plant is not to continually pluck off undesirable fruit. That doesn't deal with the nature of a tree, and it will not stop it from yielding the same undesirable fruit. The way to deal with it is to pull it out of the ground, roots and all, and plant a new tree that yields life-giving fruit.

So what did Jesus do? He went to the cross with our sinful nature. The passions and desires of our flesh were crucified with Him, according to Paul in Galatians 6. Jesus died with our old nature, pulling it up by the roots. The fruits of that nature (impurity, idolatry, enmity, and strife to name a few) withered on the vine. Then Jesus brought us into new creation, planted by streams of living water, yielding fruit in season. And what is this life-giving fruit? The fruit of the Spirit is love, joy, peace, patience, kindness, goodness, gentleness, faithfulness, and self-control. Against such things there is no law.

1 John 1:9...It's Not What You Think

In the discussion of sin and forgiveness, 1 John 1:9 certainly gets a lot of attention. I memorized it at a young age, as I suspect many people raised in the church have. Not only was this my go-to verse for trying to deal with my own struggles, it was the verse I used any time I offered counsel to others getting pummeled by sin. Hopefully the verse has come to mind as you have read this book and wondered how it fits in with all I have proposed. The verse says:

"If we confess our sins, He is faithful and just to forgive us our sins and to cleanse us from all unrighteousness."

The words are beautiful and hopeful and speak of the amazing grace of God. I love this verse. In my life, however, the misinterpretation of this verse kept me in spiritual bondage for years. No other single verse more informed my belief system than this one, especially in a doctrinal environment that was more sin-focused than grace-focused, more self-centered than Christ-centered.

1 John was a letter written to the church, and like a thorough and considerate communicator, John does not pre-suppose that everyone who hears or reads the letter is a believer. He provides a recap of the Gospel through the first chapter, contrasting those walking in light with those walking in darkness and those who carry the truth inside with those deceiving themselves. I do not believe verse 9 is instruction to believers, but rather John instructs the unsaved readers of his letter how to accept the forgiveness offered at the cross, be freed from sin and cleansed from all unrighteousness.

Friend, if you are on the hamster wheel of chasing forgiveness and striving for righteousness, get off now! Not only does such obsessive attention to sin take all your strength, it takes your focus off Jesus, and above all, it is *not getting you anywhere!* You are forgiven! You are in the right because of your faith in Jesus! What can you do to cancel God's proclamation over you? How many times must God cleanse you of *all* unrighteousness? Can we agree that God does it right the first time? Can we agree that putting the burden of staying right with God on ourselves is to treat the Good News of Jesus as though it were a mere addendum to the Old Covenant? Can we also agree that if daily, hourly, or even moment-by-moment confession of sins in order to be forgiven is indeed what John is prescribing, then we are taking a quantum leap backwards from the Old Covenant which absolved the Israelites of their sins for an entire year on the Day of Atonement?

Now please hear me, I do not take issue with a child of God acknowledging and confessing a sin before the Lord. I do not take issue with a remorseful cry from a heavy heart. But what I emphatically oppose is the false doctrine that constant confession is a condition of maintaining your forgiveness and your righteousness. That is a suffocating form of religion that depends as much on your vigilance as it does on God's goodness. If you belong to that school of thought, let me pose a few questions to you. I even challenge you to write your answers down and back them up with scripture. Please answer these questions for your own sake: How frequently do you confess your sins? Are you not forgiven if you do not confess? Do you confess all of your sins, or just the ones you remember? Do you define sin as transgressions against the law and the commands of the Bible or does your definition also include sins of omission, sins you don't know you're committing, and the biggest of all, anything that is not faith? Can you make a general confession of your sins daily, or do you need to be specific? What if you forget to confess something? What happens if you die with unconfessed sin in your life?

What happens if you do not confess at all? Remember, the New Covenant scriptures refute the absurd notion of broken fellowship with God (Romans 6:10).

Please know I am not trying to be contentious. As God is my witness, I sincerely wish to help those of you stuck in a religious rut. Had I asked myself these questions sooner, I would have been off the hamster wheel and on to greater things long ago. Now, though I have not asked for forgiveness in over 20 years, I know I am forgiven. I do not continually ask to be cleansed of all unrighteousness. I have been cleansed. I have been covered by the righteousness of Jesus and filled with His Holy Spirit. I know by faith. I have reckoned it to be true.

And confession? Confession is agreement with God. At salvation, I agreed with Him that I was a sinner who needed His gift of new life. Once I received His salvation, His forgiveness, and His Spirit, I started making new creation confessions to remind myself of all that's changed and to agree with my Father on who I am in Him.

The Intimacy of Confession

My dear friend Sherry Green (Tom's wife) once shared an insight that really opened my eyes. She said that some people feel the most intimate with God while confessing sin. There is something powerful about being reminded in the midst of your sorrow of God's goodness and faithfulness. Even when we're being swallowed up by guilt and shame, we remember the redeeming work of Jesus and call out to Him for mercy. Friend, I have more good news for you. It's possible to experience wonderful intimacy with Jesus without being bludgeoned by stone tablets or torn apart in self-flagellation. Recall that among the glories of the New Covenant is that its ministry brings life, not death! That's not to say I don't relate to the experience of accepting forgiveness in a moment of shame. It's probably very similar to the relief and gratitude felt by the woman caught in the act of adultery.

It's one of my favorite stories in all of scripture. Jesus was teaching in the temple, and the Pharisees interrupted His teaching to try and put Jesus in a tight spot. With the adulterous woman on display in the midst of them, they reminded Jesus that Moses commanded such women to be stoned, and asked His opinion. What was Jesus to do? If He disagreed with Moses, the Pharisees would accuse Him of rejecting the conditions of the covenant between God and His people. His credibility as a prophet would be shot. If He were to approve her execution, He would lose the regard of His followers along with His reputation of being a compassionate friend of sinners. They had cornered Jesus, or so they thought. But how many times in our own experiences have we seen God bypass our "either/or" options and deal with the conditions of our hearts?

Jesus would not be cornered. He initially didn't even answer their question, but stooped down and wrote in the dust with his finger. They persisted and He spoke the immortal words, "Let him who has no sin throw the first stone."

Jesus knelt down again to write in the dust. What He wrote is one of the great mysteries of scripture. One by one, beginning with the oldest, they dropped their stones and went away. Jesus, the only one who could justifiably stone this woman, did not condemn her. He only exhorted her to "go and sin no more."

Why do I love that story so much? It's not only because Jesus sidestepped the trap and redirected the misguided focus of the judgmental Pharisees to their own wickedness. It's not only because Jesus showed extreme compassion to a woman under a death sentence. I love it because this story is about you and me being caught in our shame and taken before God by the Accuser of the brethren, who threw the Law at us and demanded of God a reckoning for our sin lest His justice and righteousness be compromised. I love it because it foreshadows the reckoning for our sin through Jesus. I love it because we soon learned the woman's sin did not go unpunished, nor did the Pharisees, nor did yours or mine. When Jesus wrote in the dust, he was not sweeping transgressions under the rug. God's justice and righteousness were upheld as his innocent Son was nailed to the cross. The ground the Accuser had to stand on crumbled under his feet as Jesus cried out, "It is finished!" The stone that sealed His tomb was rolled away, crushing the head of the Enemy! And now, as Paul joyously asks in Romans 8, who can bring a charge against God's elect? It is God who justifies! Who condemns us?

Confessing Our Sins to One Another

So what place does confession of sins have in the life of the believer after receiving the gifts of forgiveness and second birth? Once we accept that confession of sins is not the condition for retaining forgiveness and righteousness, we see its important and necessary applications elsewhere.

James 5:16 instructs us to confess our sins to one another and pray for each other that we may be healed. I believe James is not only talking about coming clean for the wrongs we commit against each other (which is essential), but also sharing our secret struggles of sin with one another that we may receive prayer, encouragement, exhortation, and above all, healing. Bringing a dark struggle into the light severely depletes its strength. A confession of sin and a cry for help brings swift aid from the saints. Remember that we are created to be in the community of family, and that a family has regard and concern for their own. Those who strive in self-righteousness and pride themselves in their pious accomplishments are often uncaring and judgmental when a broken person calls for help (and also less likely to call for help themselves), but we who have been healed by the love and grace of God are quick to show it to others. If you wrong a brother, confess to him and ask his forgiveness. If you are being swallowed by sin, break its power over you by calling out. Help is already on the way.

If you feel you've insulted the grace of God too many times, that your willful insistence on sinning has prevented you from receiving any measure of kindness, repent! Turn away from the road to destruction. Even one step in the opposite direction is a step towards life. Believe that you have been forgiven, accept it, and walk in it. Put your eyes back on Jesus, and let His Holy Spirit supernaturally transform you and give you victory over the strongholds in your life.

The Word on Forgiveness

I have compiled a list of atonement verses with which to encourage you. This is by no means an exhaustive list of New Covenant scriptures, but hopefully it will spur you on to dig into God's Word and let His truth renew your mind.

"As far as the east is from the west, so far does He remove our transgressions from us." Psalm 103:12

"The next day [John] saw Jesus coming toward him, and said, 'Behold, the Lamb of God, who takes away the sin of the world!" John 1:29

"This is my blood of the covenant, which is poured out for many for the forgiveness of sins." Matthew 26:28

"[Jesus] is the propitiation for our sins, and not for ours only but also for the sins of the whole world." 1 John 2:2

"All this is from God, who through Christ reconciled us to Himself and gave us the ministry of reconciliation; that is, in

Christ God was reconciling the world to Himself, not counting their trespasses against them, and entrusting to us the message of reconciliation." 2 Corinthians 5:18-19

"In [God] we have redemption through His blood, the forgiveness of our trespasses, according to the riches of His grace..." Ephesians 1:7

"But God, being rich in mercy, because of the great love with which He loved us, even when we were dead in our trespasses, made us alive together with Christ—by grace you have been saved—and raised us up with Him and seated us with Him in the heavenly places in Christ Jesus, so that in the coming ages He might show the immeasurable riches of His grace in kindness toward us in Christ Jesus. For by grace you have been saved through faith. And this is not your own doing; it is the gift of God, not a result of works, so that no one may boast." Ephesians 2:5-9

"Be kind to one another, tenderhearted, forgiving one another, as God in Christ forgave you." Ephesians 4:32

"[God] has delivered us from the domain of darkness and transferred us to the kingdom of His beloved Son, in whom we have redemption, the forgiveness of sins." Colossians 1:13-14

"And you, who were dead in your trespasses and the uncircumcision of your flesh, God made alive together with Him, having forgiven us all our trespasses, by canceling the record of debt that stood against us with its legal demands. This He set aside, nailing it to the cross." Colossians 2:13-14

"Put on then, as God's chosen ones, holy and beloved, compassionate hearts, kindness, humility, meekness, and patience, bearing with one another and, if one has a complaint against another, forgiving each other; as the Lord has forgiven you, so you also must forgive." Colossians 3:12-13

"[Jesus] is the radiance of the glory of God and the exact imprint of His nature, and He upholds the universe by the word of His power. After making purification for sins, He sat down at the right hand of the Majesty on high, having become as much superior to angels as the name He has inherited is more excellent than theirs." Hebrews 1:3-4

"But as it is, [Jesus] has appeared once for all at the end of the ages to put away sin by the sacrifice of Himself." Hebrews 9:26b

"But when Christ had offered for all time a single sacrifice for sins, He sat down at the right hand of God, waiting from that time until His enemies should be made a footstool for His feet. For by a single offering He has perfected for all time those who are being sanctified." Hebrews 10:12-14

"'I will remember their sins and their lawless deeds no more.' Where there is forgiveness of these, there is no longer any offering for sin." Hebrews 10:17-18

"Grace to you and peace from Him who is and who was and who is to come, and from the seven spirits who are before His throne, and from Jesus Christ the faithful witness, the firstborn of the dead, and the ruler of kings on earth. To Him who loves us and has freed us from our sins by His blood and made us a kingdom, priests to His God and Father, to Him be glory and dominion forever and ever. Amen. " Revelation 1:4-6

Chapter 8
ALL THINGS NEW

So here we are, in the Promised Land. Here we are, resting in peace with God. Old things have passed away, and all things have become new. We walk in the Spirit's garden and tend the fruit. We co-labor with the Lord to see His kingdom come fully on earth, as it is in heaven. Day by day, we grow in the likeness and image of Jesus.

Among the first scripture passages I cherished as a young boy was Hebrews 12:1-3. It speaks of being surrounded by a great cloud of witnesses, of throwing off the sin that trips us up, and about running the race set out in front of us, all the while keeping our eyes on Jesus, the author and finisher of our faith.

The Apostle Paul uses the imagery of running a race several times in his epistles. In my former way of thinking, I morphed the symbolism and missed the Gospel. I believed the prize was to one day achieve a status of righteousness, or right standing, with God. I knew I couldn't be perfect, but I could certainly be doing a lot better.

Then the Lord opened my eyes to this truth: righteousness is not our finish line; it's our starting block. We begin in Christ in right standing with our Father. We begin as those reconciled to God. We begin by being justified. We begin by being sanctified (set apart for holy use). From that place of victory, we start the race. Runners in this race are New Covenant, new creation people. It's time to leave the old behind.

What's New?

In John's vision recorded in Revelation 21, he sees the Lord Jesus seated on the throne, making this declaration: "Behold, I am making all things new." Everything has changed for those who are born of the Holy Spirit:

We have a new heart (Ezekiel 36:26).

We have a new identity (2 Corinthians 5:17&21).

We have a new Father (Romans 8:15).

We have a new mother (Galatians 4:31).

We have a new spouse (Romans 7:4).

We have new brothers and sisters (Hebrews 2:11).

We have new roots (Colossians 2:6-12).

We have a new ancestry and lineage (Romans 5:18-19).

We have a new job description (2 Corinthians 5:18-20).

We have a new purpose (Ephesians 2:10).

We have new power (Ephesians 3:20-21).

We have new motivation (Philippians 2:13).

We have new fruit (Galatians 5:22-23).

You were a sinner, now you are a saint. You had a depraved mind, now you have the mind of Christ. You were under judgment and condemnation, now you are justified. Your disobedience led to sin and death, but Christ's obedience has made you righteous. You were under law, now you are under grace. You were dead and separated from God, now you are alive and living in unbroken fellowship with Him. You were a slave to sin, now you are a slave to righteousness. You were an orphan, now you are a child of God. You once existed in the kingdom of darkness, now you belong to the kingdom of the Son of His love.

What's Next?

If the summation of your Christian experience to this point has been staying out of trouble, and when that doesn't work, cleaning up your mess when you do get into trouble, there is so much more to look forward to. Repentance from dead works is elementary, according to Hebrews 6. It's time to advance in the abundant life Jesus came to give you. It's time to embrace the Good News. It's time to be transformed by the renewing of your mind. It's time to walk in newness of life with the fullness of the Godhead dwelling within you. It's time to plumb the unsearchable depths of His Spirit with the mind of Christ that you have been given. It's time to walk victoriously as more than a conqueror, to resist the Devil and watch him run, and to wield the weapons of the Spirit and pull down the Enemy's strongholds. It's time to view yourself as an able minister of the New Covenant, possessing everything you need for life and godliness. It's time to serve as an ambassador of the Kingdom of Heaven and reclaim ground taken from you, from those you love, and from those you encounter by chance or by routine. It's time to be the fragrance of Heaven. It's time to proclaim liberty to the captives, to open the doors of those in prisons, to open the eyes of the blind, to declare the acceptable time of the Lord. Following Jesus is about so much more than an afterlife destination; it's about your present reality as a Kingdom ambassador and your ministry of bringing heaven to earth in your family, your neighborhood, your workplace, your school.

Beyond the Veil

In the Old Covenant, King Solomon built a temple for the Lord. At the dedication of the temple, 22,000 cattle and 120,000 sheep and goats were sacrificed. The Holy of Holies represented the dwelling place of God, and it was separated from the rest of the temple by a thick veil. That veil remained until Jesus satisfied the legal requirements and penalties of the Old Covenant on the cross and declared, "It is finished!" At that moment, the veil in the temple was torn, from top to bottom, from heaven to earth, and the way into the Most Holy Place was left wide open. Hebrews 10:20 says the battered body of Jesus is the torn veil through which we have now entered the most holy presence of God.

Soon after the ascension of Jesus, the Spirit of God came in power on the day of Pentecost, which, not coincidentally, was the day Israel celebrated the receiving of the Mosaic Law and began on earth an eternal era of God's kingdom under the New Covenant. The Old Covenant's pillar of fire in the midst of the wilderness masses, showing the consuming power of God but denying access and intimacy, was replaced by tongues of flame over the head of each believer, a sign that the Spirit of God now made the hearts of new creation His dwelling place on earth.

The Old Covenant showed a governance of the nation through the law. The New Covenant shows a governance of the individual by the indwelling Holy Spirit. This was prophesied by Jeremiah and repeated in Hebrews 8. No longer would a man tell another to know the Lord, for they would all know Him. His law would be written on their hearts and minds, not on stones of condemnation. He would remember their sins and transgressions no more. He would be their God, and they would be His people. This prophecy foretold the end of the Old Covenant (Hebrews 8:13) and the establishing of the New Covenant, ratified by the blood of Jesus, enjoyed by the new creation race.

This is the Good News the prophets longed to see. We are the temple of the Lord. We are carriers of the Spirit of God. As Solomon cleansed the temple with the blood of animals, the blood of Jesus has cleansed us, that His Spirit might inhabit us! To what end? That we may know Him and make Him known in the earth. To expand the Kingdom of God on earth as it is in heaven. No longer confined to a single structure made by man, the Spirit has multiplied His presence, making it possible for people from every nation, tribe, and tongue to encounter Him. Now your friends, family, neighbors, co-workers, grocery store clerks, accountants, gas station attendants, fellow restaurant patrons, anybody and everybody that crosses your path can encounter God through you, by His Spirit living inside you.

Sadly, you'll remember that one of the Enemy's schemes is to use our fear, judgment, disdain or disapproval of others to cause us to put a veil over the Spirit in our lives, restricting others' access to Him (the scheme of putting our eyes on others). Looking at people from a worldly point of view (which Paul speaks against in 2 Corinthians 5:16) has too often prevented us from reaching out to those in desperate need of a life-changing encounter with God. God removed the veil restricting our access to Him; let us also move beyond the veil to let the world see Him clearly in our lives.

Who Do You Love?

What credit is it to you, Jesus asked, to love those who love you? Do not even the heathen do that? The love we have been called to express is not elitist. It is not for certain demographics, people groups, political parties, social classes, religions, gender identities, or sexual orientations. We do not need to screen potential candidates to see who is worthy to receive divine love. All we need to do is remember the amazing grace and love God offered us while we were enemies in our minds with Him, opposed to Him and His ways, and to remember how that love brought miraculous change in our lives.

Not only is love the defining characteristic of God, it is what defines us as Christians. Jesus said it Himself; "The world will know you are my followers if you love one another." Jesus also said the one who loves God keeps His commandments, the two greatest being love God and love your neighbor as yourself. The Apostle John writes one of the most beautiful passages about love:

"So we have come to know and to believe the love that God has for us. God is love, and whoever abides in love abides in God, and God abides in Him. By this is love perfected with us, so that we may have confidence for the day of judgment, because as he is so also are we in this world. There is no fear in love, but perfect love casts out fear. For fear has to do with punishment, and whoever fears has not been perfected in love. We love because He first loved us. If anyone says, "I love God," and hates his brother, he is a liar; for he who does not love his brother whom he has seen cannot love God whom he has not seen. And this commandment we have from Him: whoever loves God must also love his brother." 1 John 4:16-21

Love is the chief identifying mark of the followers of Jesus. The commandments, according to Jesus, are summed up in this: love God with all your heart, mind, soul, and strength, and love your neighbor as yourself. Jesus also said in John 14:23 that the one who loves Him is the one who keeps His commands, so the case can be made that we cannot love God without loving our neighbor as ourselves. Paul lists some amazing feats one can achieve through the power of the Spirit in 1 Corinthians 13, but declares that without love it comes to nothing. Your love for someone may very well be regarded as an endorsement of his or her destructive choices or an approval of the broken identity they have embraced. *Love them anyway.* Love covers a multitude of sins. The love of Jesus can soften the hardest heart and cause repentance in even the most wayward soul. Consider Zacchaeus.

Jesus and Zacchaeus

"Zacchaeus was a wee little man, and a wee little man was he." I sang these words as a child in Sunday School, and I really identified with the story (you will recall I was a wee little man for quite some time). But the story took on special significance as I grew in my understanding of the grace of Jesus.

Those who hungered for justice held Zacchaeus at bay. He was a swindler, and what's worse, he stole from his own people to make himself rich while sharing the bounty with the pagan Roman Empire occupying Israel. His countrymen, enflamed with anger and hatred towards such a traitor, may have had to share their hard-earned wages with him, but they did not have to share with him this Rabbi Jesus everyone was talking about.

And yet Zacchaeus wanted to see Jesus. He, too, hungered for compassion, for salvation. The crowds would surely push him aside, and he was small in stature, so he climbed a sycamore tree just to get a glimpse. And Jesus made a beeline for him.

"Zacchaeus, come down from there right now," Jesus said. "I must stay at your house."

The crowds muttered exactly as I would have muttered. How many of them must have longed to have Jesus as their houseguest? They felt the sting of such an unjust act, this kindness shown to an unworthy recipient. They indignantly complained about Jesus associating with Zacchaeus, such a well-documented sinner. No doubt some were perplexed at how Jesus could seem to be the Messiah and yet show such partiality to a lawbreaker. Surely the Messiah would come and drive out the occupiers, punish the traitors, and exalt the covenant-keepers. Surely His arm would bring justice to the nations. But this Jesus was extending his arm to Zacchaeus, not in wrath, but in kindness.

Justice came, but in a way no one in the disgruntled crowd expected. Justice, galvanized by divine love, came in the words of a newly repentant tax collector. "Lord, I now give half of my wealth to the poor, and I will repay four times any I have cheated."

"Salvation has come to this house," Jesus said to the crowd.

Astounding.

Jesus accomplished in one brief invitation, one empowering gesture of friendship, what scores of condemning words, bitter looks, and clenched fists could never do. He changed a heart of stone to a heart of flesh. He looked past the flaws, which was all the crowd could see, and saw a lost sheep wishing to return home. All Jesus had to do was call his name, and Zacchaeus found his way back. Don't miss the fact that grace was shown not only to Zacchaeus, but to those in the crowd who had been wronged by him as his repentance brought about restitution to those he'd cheated.

Jesus and the (Poor) Rich Young Ruler

Contrast the story of Zacchaeus with another account of a man seeking Jesus. In the story of the rich young ruler from Luke 18, we see a man playing by the rules. We see a man who is highly esteemed in society. We see a man who has kept the law since he was old enough to do so. We see a rich, young ruler who received his wealth, as the others saw it, because he was "living right."

This man approached Jesus and asked, "Good teacher, what must I do to inherit eternal life?" I always found Jesus's response a curious one. He said there was no one good except God. Wasn't Jesus good? Why would He say that? Why would He deflect this man's assessment of Him?

Jesus began listing the commandments of the Mosaic code, which the man assured Jesus he'd obeyed since a young boy. Jesus then told him to sell all he had and give it to the poor, and come follow Him. The man could not do it and went away in sorrow.

Jesus rejected the religious standards of the day that determined if something was good or evil. God was good, and His law was good, but man was not, regardless of how closely they adhered to the Old Covenant. Jesus questioned man's flawed definition of "good" as it was based on personal performance and achievement, not on reliance upon God. He recognized the basis of the young man's question was to see what needed to be achieved to inherit eternal life. The crowd was perplexed and anxious and wondered who could be saved, if not people like the rich ruler. Jesus uttered the famous phrase, "What is impossible with man is possible with God."

So Zacchaeus, the well-known treacherous sinner, inherited eternal life, yet the upright, law-abiding young ruler went away in sorrow. What does this tell you about coming into the Kingdom of God? It requires a new approach to living. It requires a new mindset. It requires rebirth. It requires new creation. It requires His Spirit.

Do we see ourselves in these stories? I see myself, for sure. I am with the crowd passing judgements on the worthiness of the rich man and the unworthiness of the traitor. I wait for Jesus to offer praise to the rich ruler and scathing rebuke to Zacchaeus. I am shocked when the scoundrel is rewarded and the highly esteemed goes away sorrowful. But whose name is written down? Both sought Him, yet only one ended up with Jesus. The transformed Zacchaeus emptied his hands and received a full heart, while the unchanged rich man went away empty-hearted with full hands. And that leaves us in the crowd to puzzle over the justice of Jesus.

A valuable thing to note in these two stories is that both men were looking for Jesus, and both had opportunities to give away their wealth, yet it was the "righteous" man who could not and the sinner who gladly did. Jesus showed love to both, but only Zacchaeus let that love in to do a work in his heart. The effect in Zacchaeus's life was to spread the generosity Jesus had shown him to his fellow man. As Pastor Alan says, the Christian life is receiving and giving.

Maggie's Flower

When my firstborn child Maggie was just a toddler, I took her for a quick trip to the park down the street from our home. Maggie contentedly rode in her stroller, surveying the world with the childlike wonder we adults wish we still had. Halfway to the park, she shouted, "Flower!" and pointed at some vibrant yellow dandelions growing out of the sidewalk. I plucked one and handed it to her. Maggie's attention was riveted on her new prize as she clutched the flower firmly in her hand. At the park Maggie continued to hold on to her precious flower, even while swinging or going down the slide.

As we were preparing to leave, a younger, wobblier girl saw Maggie and her flower, and with the balance of a newborn fawn made her way over to us. As she drew near, her eyes locked on Maggie's flower. And then a remarkable thing happened. Maggie slowly and carefully extended the flower as a gift to the girl, and my eyes grew wide in amazement at Maggie's generosity. Suddenly, my daughter retracted her hand before the girl could take it. The girl looked anxiously at Maggie, who looked anxiously at me. I knelt down next to Maggie and reassuringly placed my hand on her back.

"Maggie, if you want to give her your flower, I will get you another one." Maggie nodded, faced the little girl, and handed her the flower. The girl happily received it and wobbled away with Maggie forlornly watching her. We played a little longer, and as we started to leave, I noticed the little girl watching us.

"Maggie, do you want to say goodbye?" I asked. Maggie turned back and paused for a moment before speaking.

"Bye-bye, flower."

God's grace frees us from our tendency to hoard good things for ourselves. He tells us to take enough bread for the day, as there is an endless supply for those who trust Him. He provided for you yesterday. He is your provision today, tomorrow, and forever. Our Father knows all we need before we ask and often gives us blessings before we realize we need them. He knows how to give good things to His children. You can never out-give Him. He gives to bless and He also gives so we can experience the blessing of giving to others. But realize you cannot give love if you have not accepted God's love for you. You cannot forgive if you haven't accepted God's forgiveness for yourself.

Confessions of New Creation

Since your voice is the one you are most likely to listen to, you must reject what you think and say about yourself when it doesn't align with God's proclamations. If confession is agreeing with God, then renew your mind and begin making new creation confessions:

I have been crucified with Christ (Galatians 2:20).

I have been baptized into Jesus' death, burial, and resurrection (Romans 6:3-4).

I have been adopted by God as His own child (Romans 8:15).

I have been raised up by God and seated with Him in heavenly places in Christ (Ephesians 2:6).

I am new creation (2 Corinthians 5:17).

I am a minister of reconciliation (2 Corinthians 5:18).

I am an ambassador for Christ (2 Corinthians 5:20).

I am transformed by the renewing of my mind (Romans 12:2).

I have the mind of Christ (1 Corinthians 2:16).

I am a child of God, an heir with God, and a co-heir with Jesus (Romans 8:17).

I am more than a conqueror through Him who loves me (Romans 8:37).

I have everything I need for life and godliness (2 Peter 1:3).

God works in me to will and act according to His purpose (Philippians 2:13).

I am God's temple and His Spirit dwells in me (1 Corinthians 3:16).

I am an able minister of the New Covenant (2 Corinthians 3:6).

I am an overcomer, and greater is He who is in me than he who is in the world (1 John 4:4).

I belong to a chosen race, a royal priesthood, a holy nation, for God's possession (1 Peter 2:9).

Fixing Our Eyes on Jesus

In the second chapter of this book, I discussed the schemes of the Enemy to take our eyes from Jesus. At this point you've learned how the glorious Gospel of Jesus frees us from these traps.

When the Enemy tries to put our eyes on the command, we remind ourselves that the law of the Spirit of life in Christ has set us free from the law of sin and death (Romans 8:2). When the Enemy tries to put our eyes on a lie, we continue looking at Jesus; the Way, the Truth, and the Life (John 14:6). We know the truth and it sets us free (John 8:32). When the Enemy points out lack, we stand in the truth that we have everything we need for life and godliness (2 Peter 1:3). When the Enemy points out an object of temptation, we remember that no temptation has seized us except what is common to man, that God will not let us be tempted beyond what we can bear, and that He is faithful to provide the way of escape that we may endure any temptation (1 Corinthians 10:13). We remember that Christ was also tempted in every way but was without sin, and we rejoice that the same Spirit of Jesus dwells within us. When the Enemy attacks us with shame, we lift our heads and proclaim that there is no condemnation for those who are in Christ Jesus (Romans 8:1). We hold fast to the Gospel proclamation that God is for us, that God justified us, and that the Enemy cannot bring a charge against us or condemn us. We take comfort in knowing that Jesus is interceding for us (Romans 8:31-34). Finally, when the Enemy tries to put our eyes on others, we no longer regard them according to the flesh or judge them by fleshly standards (2 Corinthians 5:16). We see them as family, or as people in need of family, and we implore them to be reconciled to their Father (2 Corinthians 5:20).

Against all these schemes, we fix our eyes on Jesus, the pioneer and perfecter of our faith (Hebrews 12:2). As we behold the glory of the Lord, we are transformed into His image from glory to glory (2 Corinthians 3:18).

We Become What We Behold

"That boy is the spitting image of his father, a real chip off the old block!" We hear sentiments like this expressed often. Children resemble their parents, not only because of genetics, but because they look up to them and study them so much in childhood that they begin to pick up their traits and mannerisms. In the same way, whatever image or idea of God we hold to, we reflect to others. The way we treat and regard others is a direct indicator of our beliefs on God's treatment and regard for us.

If God appears harsh and distant to us, we are harsh and distant to others. If God appears critical and judgmental, we show criticism and judgment to others. If we believe God's love and favor must be earned, we make others work for our love and favor. If God is vindictive, angry, and wrathful, we display the same attributes.

Our God is defined by love. He is the eternal source of mercy and grace. He used His blood to ratify the New Covenant. God sealed this covenant by unsealing the tomb where Jesus's dead body lay. God took away the stone covering the tomb, and He took away our stony hearts to replace them with hearts of flesh, His life-giving law written on them. God brought into existence a new race of men by filling the man Jesus with His Holy Spirit and raising him from the dead. Jesus, the firstborn from the dead, calls to those dead in trespasses and sins and lying in the tomb, "Come forth." By faith, we come. By faith, we leave those rotten grave clothes behind, and we carry not the stench of death, but the beautiful fragrance of heaven.

Jesus said in John 14:9, "If you have seen me, you have seen the Father." We worship the Lord, in spirit and in truth, and as we behold Him, we become what we behold, from one degree of glory to another, until we see Him face to face and know Him as we are known. Turn your eyes to Jesus. Despite the constant schemes of the Enemy, keep your eyes on Jesus. Behold the man.

Jesus, the visible expression of the invisible God,

Jesus, the author and finisher of our faith,

Jesus, through whom came grace and truth,

Jesus, the Good Shepherd,

Jesus, the Lamb of God who took away the sin of the world,

Jesus, who endured the cross, scorning its shame, for the joy to come,

Jesus, who was wounded for our transgressions, bruised for our iniquities,

Jesus, the propitiation for our sins,

Jesus, our High Priest, who used His own blood to forever cleanse us,

Jesus, the only intermediary between God and men,

Jesus, whose obedience has the power to present all men righteous to God,

Jesus, the first-born from the dead,

Jesus, the mediator of a better covenant,

Jesus, in whom the promises of God find their "yes" and "amen",

Jesus, in whom lies hidden all the treasures of wisdom and knowledge,

Jesus, able to save to the uttermost those who draw near to God through Him,

Jesus, in whom we live and move and have our being,

Jesus.

Deep Calls Unto Deep

I will close this book with a story from my own experience. In 2004, my wife and I had an amazing opportunity to visit my dear friend Rocky Green, who was living on the Hawaiian island of Oahu. Rocky had a job leading worship at a church, lived in a small apartment above the church, and drove an old Cadillac with a surf rack on top. It was a joyous and relatively frugal vacation, staying in his apartment, riding around the island in his DeVille, and going to all the secret spots most tourists did not know about.

Midway through the trip, Rocky took me and Becky (about three months pregnant with our youngest daughter) to a famous body-surfing spot called Makapu'u Beach. While Becky was relaxing on the beach, Rocky and I played in the surf. Having very little beach experience at that time, I was unaware of the foolishness of standing in the waves with my back turned to the ocean. I learned my lesson the hard way when a crashing wave knocked me off my feet and put me through the spin cycle. When I recovered and came up for air, water to my waist, I noticed I was further from shore, but before I could remedy this, a second wave knocked me down. I came up gasping, even further from shore, water to my chest and starting to panic, when a third wave broke upon me. Adrenaline surged as I

148

desperately swam for shore with all my might, and when I made it to dry ground, I exhaustedly collapsed on the sand beside Becky. Neither she nor Rocky had witnessed my ordeal, and Becky hopped up and ran to the water. In just a short while, I noticed she was in the same predicament. I jumped up and started moving toward the water just as she called for help.

"ROCKY!" she shouted. Rocky was already in the water, and being a surfer and former lifeguard, he knew how to handle the situation. I still recall my admiration as his arms cut through the waves with strong and confident strokes, and I was put at ease by the smile on his face, reassuring Becky that he had her and she would be fine. I am not only thankful that Rocky saved my wife and unborn child, I'm thankful that Becky called his name instead of mine, or else she and I both would have been in a lot of trouble!

Near the end of our trip, Rocky wanted to show us a great snorkeling spot. He was really looking forward to it, so I did my best to hide my lack of enthusiasm, shaken as I still was by the danger of our earlier episode. When we got to the beach, Rocky handed me a mask and snorkel, put his own on, and pointed to a reef sticking out of the water about thirty yards from shore. Off he went, happily diving into the water and swimming out to investigate. I looked back at Becky, comfortably (and safely) lying on her towel, then back at the foreboding water. I waded out until the water was at my knees, then I stopped.

I must have stood there for about ten minutes. I didn't have the courage to swim out to the reef, but I had too much pride to go back to shore. I gave myself pep talks and searched for motivation, but all for naught. Finally, Rocky swam back. I started fiddling with my mask and snorkel, unconvincingly pretending my progress had been delayed by an ill-fitting strap.

"Wow, there are some cool things to see over there," he said. "Are you okay?"

I hesitated, but pushed through my embarrassment. "I guess I'm still rattled from the experience at Makapu'u."

"I totally understand," Rocky said. "Well, you know how to swim, right?"

"Yeah," I warily replied.

"And you know how to float if you get tired, right?"

"I suppose so."

"Then you're good!" he said with a smile, though the look on my face told him I wasn't yet persuaded. "Look," he said, "I'll swim out with you. I'll be right beside you the whole time, in case you get in trouble."

"What are you going to do if I get in trouble?" I asked dubiously.

"If you get tired, I'll hold you up." As I visualized the picture of Rocky holding me up while I flailed in the ocean, my new priority became the preservation of my reputation and dignity. At that point, I would sooner drown than be thought of by Rocky as someone who couldn't take care of himself (I suppose if I did drown, I couldn't avoid being thought of as someone who couldn't take care of himself).

"Let's go," I said. With no resistance other than my nervousness, we swam out. As soon as we reached the reef, I latched on to the shore-side of it, using its mass as a shield from the incoming waves. I felt relatively safe and clung tightly to the reef while sticking my face under the water to see what I could. Rocky snorkeled into open water along the backside of the reef. I was completely content with this arrangement until Rocky returned to my side a few minutes later. He excitedly removed his mask.

"Come over to the other side. There's something I think you'll want to see for yourself." His invitation momentarily put me in another crisis of courage. I would have to let go of my security and follow him into open water, unprotected from the waves. But the look of assurance in his eyes, coupled with how far I'd already come, prompted me to trust him and let go. I followed him around the side, and as soon as we cleared the reef, I saw what Rocky had been excited about. A majestic, giant sea turtle slowly paddled through the water just a few feet in front us (a Green Turtle, known in the native dialect as "Honu"). I smiled as big as I could without losing my snorkel. The turtle swam around us, close enough to touch, and the sunlight refracting through the waves beautifully highlighted the colors and patterns on its shell. For several minutes, we passed the time in blissful observation, the turtle paying no mind to our presence. In a shoebox somewhere is a photo of the moment, snapped by Rocky with an underwater camera, of the turtle and me sharing the ocean. It was truly a glorious experience. When the turtle finally swam away, I realized that I had completely forgotten about my fear.

I have reflected on that story many times since Rocky's passing. I have puzzled over why Rocky didn't say, "Come over here and look at this giant sea turtle!" I would not have hesitated to act if he'd said that. My best guess is Rocky wanted to allow me the thrill of discovery, he wanted to show himself trustworthy, and he wanted me to move out in faith. Just like Jesus.

And so, friend, the invitation is extended to you today. Jesus loves you with a perfect love. His love is unchanging, even if you decide to stay on the shore and observe the surface of the deep from afar. But He has readied you for life in a new realm, a life known only to those who are born of Him. If you'll trust Him, He'll take you deeper. He will teach you to live and move, even in an environment you don't feel suited or equipped for. Listen to His admonition, "Do not be afraid." Push away the fear and follow Him into the deep.

You are going to get weary from time to time, but don't worry. You can always depend on Him. He's right beside you every bit of the way. When your strength fails, He'll hold you up.

Deep calls unto deep. Jesus beckons. He will show you new and wonderful things. Things you cannot see from the shore. The old is behind you, the new is before you. A New Covenant. A new creation. A new realm. A new way of life. A new you.

All things new.

This is the last page of the book. Are you disappointed?
Don't be.

On to abundant life.

40099265R00088

Made in the USA
San Bernardino, CA
11 October 2016